ISBN: 978-1-329-44768-4

Cover art courtesy of Joyce Doris

A Book I'll Never Write

For those who could not find the words themselves

Colors of Coping

Once I was white as coffee cream
Not quite pure, but not unclean
Now I'm blacker than the crow
In the shade of Death's shadow
Couples walking hand in hand
Make me green as false gold bands
While on lonely nights when I can't sleep
I'm bluer than the tears I weep
Unserved justice paints me red
Red as blood, blood you bled
I'm yellow as the sun on high
To think of all the years still nigh
I'm pink and orange and brown at night
Where dreams still see you here, alive
But when I wake and face the day
You're gone and I am only gray

Physical Memories

I wake up and you're there
But you're not
Your presence is pressed into the sheets at my side
I trail my hand through the warm hollow
And a thousand nocturnal memories assault me
Smiling, I get up
But I'm still there
A silky silhouette intertwined with yours
This morning I don't think I'll fix the bed
I'll just lie in with you

In Accordance

My heart and my head have differing views
But neither is wrong so which should I choose
My head says run, my heart says fly
My head asks what, my heart asks why
My head says can't, my heart says won't
My head says try, my heart says don't
My head says think, my heart says feel
My head says wait, my heart says deal
My head looks out, my heart looks in
My head asks how, my heart asks when
Two contrasting powers: my head and my heart
So easy to tell their opinions apart
But there's always one subject they concur to be true
They have no doubt that I love you

Don't Go

DOn't go;
RAchel please don't leave
ME; I want to be a good husband and a good
FAther, but it's hard to stay
SOber; I can't just switch to
LAttes; without you on my
TEam I know I'll just
DOte on the bottle ignoring the
TEetotal lifestyle you hoped to
LAud into my foolish nature; I need the
SOlace you provide to right me when I
FAll; I promise I'll try harder to make ends
MEet because I love you
RAchel
DOn't go

Note

I never thought I'd fall to tears from a letter left by you
But all it took was one quick look to tear my heart in two
Now I sit alone in an empty house with a bottle in my hand
While a crumpled note goes up in smoke on a wrought-iron candle stand
And as the ashes fade to gray I slowly close my eyes
Knowing I just might not wake when morning lights the skies
Because life is not worth living without you loving me
I'd rather die tonight than miss your memory

Wake-Up Call

Rise and shine my darling; a new day has begun
Throw back your frilly curtains and outshine the rising sun
Cast off the shroud of sleep now and embrace the warmth of day
And let my voice caress you while I chase the night away
Rub your bleary eyes now and shake your tousled hair
Tap your feet against the floorboards and breathe deep the morning air
Look out upon the dewy grass and pasture wreathed in mist
And laugh for joy that you have seen such beauty can exist
Now open up your ears and hear the songbirds sing
And part your lips and give the world what only you can bring
Merge your voice with mine now and we'll out-sing the lark
And we'll greet the day together as we drive away the dark
Now raise your chin and stretch that smile for you have naught to mourn
You've a life to live, and me to love, and a new day's just been born

Procrastination

Is it time for me to say I love you
And If I do
Will you say you love me too
Or will you tear my words apart
With a silent blow to my feeble heart
Perhaps I'll wait another day

Dusk and Dawn

While falling asleep under star choked skies I bid the moon good night
And in reply it smiled at me with its silky silver light
Now waking up to rose hued skies and softly sunlit land
I try to tell the moon good morning, but it doesn't understand

What Am I to You

When you look at me, what do you see?
Am I your girlfriend, your soul-mate, your bride to be?
Just give me a clue
What am I to you?
Am I the breath in your lungs, the blood in your veins?
Am I the name on your lips, the thoughts in your brain?
Am I the color in your cheek, the twinkle in your eye?
Am I the tingle in your fingertips, the contentment in your sigh?
Am I the girl in your dreams, the sweetness in your tears?
Am I the taste on your tongue, the music in your ears?
Am I the tremble in your knees, the tremor in your voice?
Am I the culprit of your smile, the confidence in your choice?
Am I the shortness of your breath, the perfect in your life?
Am I the skip in your step, your girlfriend, your soul-mate, or soon to be wife?
Just what am I to you?
And maybe I'll be yours too

Evil

What is this I hear?
The end of evil is near?
Because we have destroyed the leader of the world's fear?
Well let me make something clear
All that we hold near and dear
Is sitting here
Before you
But look in a mirror
And just what appears,
But the evil you said you slew

Mixed Signals

Mixed signals, red or green
Play it safe or read between
The lines
I hear she loves me, loves me not
Should I give it all I've got
And if I do then what if she declines
Crooked finger, smile inviting
Cold shoulder, slightly slighting
Maybe I should tell her how I feel
But how do I discern what's fake or real

Bigotry

Oh for the bigotry rife in this race
Alas, common sense and decency just can't keep pace
From the pigment of skin to your gender or sex
To your sexual orientation, just what could be next
From your religious outlook, to social tier
To cultural custom, slandered by ignorance or fear
What happened to peace, what happened to love
What happens when push comes to shove
The hate just grows to epidemic proportions
Twisted and mangled to grotesque contortions
Why can't we all just get along
And see the line between right and wrong

Earth's Receding Hairline

A throng of people weep as the last tree dies
Pretending it wasn't them who threw the final blow
Now watch the craters of the moon slowly fill with tears
As it mourns the earth it used to know
All the warnings were before us, seen but oft ignored
And we chose instead to live as Nature's foe
Now I pray this message might be heard, before it is too late
And another world lives our tale of woe

Justice

Cigarette smoke swirling, one cherry red light
Folded in his trench coat, face hidden from sight
He walks along the shadowed streets, one with the night
A cool demeanor incongruous to his hands corpse white
Shaking as they draw the gun, gripping it tight
Hating what they have to do to finally set things right
A flash, a bang, a muffled thud, the deed is finally done
Street lights glint off ruby blood, smoke wafts from the gun
A picture drops to the street, a memory laid to rest
A little girl just three years old and a father who did his best
Another bang, another thud, his form falls by the first
A victim and a killer, their positions now reversed

Thunderclap

I see the storm clouds darkening, rumbling with thunder
Lightning flashing snake-like from their bellies hanging under
Watch the rain come tumbling upon the ground below
Quenching the thirst of the land as it yearns to grow
Now the creatures scurry, shelter on the mind
Watch them as they hurry for whatever they can find
Rivers flowing faster, slapping at their banks
The world comes alive to give its thanks

Tears

Tears are the liquid shards of a broken heart
Hold them in and they'll tear you apart
But letting them go can hurt just as bad
Because once they're gone
You realize they're all you ever had

Beautiful

I tried to find a flower to match the color of your hair
Only to discover that the species wasn't there
Because despite all of the amazing things that nature can do
It's never made anything quite as beautiful as you

Seclusion

If I curtained us off from the world would you finally talk to me
Would you open up your heart and let me see
Would you let me touch your scars
Mend your wounds, make them ours
Would you finally unchain your love and set it free

Seasons

Leaves of green turning gray
Silken petals, Winter's prey
Sinking, sulking, dying, dead
Earth its coffin, snow its bed
Seasons changing, beauty lost
Winter sighs, contented frost
But like a phoenix from its ash
When the Spring and Winter clash
Once again a beauty grows
A flower blooms, a blood red rose

Abyss

I'm sinking into the abyss
Oh how I'll miss the sun
The light withdraws
As I fall
I guess the darkness won
But no, just wait
It's not too late
I feel it in my heart
I have to fight
To reach the light
It's not my time to part
Because you see
Someone loves me
As much as I love her
And if I wait
Perhaps my fate
Won't grow any darker

The Coming Storm

Color blooms across the sky in twisting shades of grey
Where heavy storm clouds thicken in ephemeral disarray
Here and there sweet golden light burrows through the fray
To gild the thirsty land below with halos of hidden day
Leaves rustle in the trees as the wind begins to blow
And the banshee howl of tortured air soon begins to low
The grass appears to stretch and sway reaching for sodden skies
And at last the first drops strike their stalks and it seems the whole world sighs

Infallible

All that matters now matters not in the end
Because what you believe always depends
Upon what you know
That's just how it goes
Or at least it's believed to be so

Insomnia

I lie awake
Insomnia restraining slumber
Of course I'm thinking of you
I know the thoughts are pointless and painful
I try to shut them out
But heartache is relentless and addicting
My dreams are the only realm we're together
But waking from them paints reality grim
I refuse to sleep
I'm growing weary
In body and mind
Pain becomes familiar and I fear to slip into apathy
One day, I tell myself, as time drifts into tomorrow
One day you'll lie awake too
And I'll be there to kiss you goodnight

Victory

What do you do
When the only option left to you
Is giving in
Makes you feel bitter
Knowing you're a quitter
Even if you couldn't win
Perhaps you choose
Not to lose
Without a fight
Because it's not the winner's glory
Or the loser's shame
It's how you played the game
That says you played it right

Never Land

I sit in silent solitude
Half lit dusk painting the horizon gold
A distant glitter so far from reach
I avert my view a full half circle
Choosing the familiarity of the encroaching dark
I see my shadow stretching grotesquely
It seems disjointed from my hunched figure
My companionship abandoned even by it
I touch a thimble to my lips
Cool metal fails to substitute soft flesh
It stoically shrugs off the tears that strike its silvery surface
Never seems to be my home
Forever alone in this land without progress
A boy not yet a man

Fidelity

No matter what life throws my way
So long as you are here to stay
I'll see it through
Because nothing short of eternity
Could ever be enough for me
In terms of you

Masochist

I'm popping pills but my heart just beats quicker
I slash my wrists but my skin just grows thicker
I swallow bullets but my skull just grows stronger
I tie a noose but the rope just grows longer
I just can't seem to find the pain
To escape the one driving me insane
But the heartache and the heartbreak I have to resist
I guess that's how I became a masochist
It's not that I enjoy the pain
Nor does self-mutilation entertain
But there is safety in control
And I can govern my body if not my soul
One day, I'm sure, I'll go too far
A cut too deep, my final scar
But that's a risk I have to face
To fight the emotions I displace
Through cuts and burns and bruises too
I'm a masochist for loving you

Corrupting Paradise

I'm standing in the garden
Forbidden fruit dripping from my lips
I should be happy in paradise
But there's something amiss
I look out at a world so much darker than my own
A desert around this oasis of mine
And I fear those sands are slipping in
That they'll consume this garden if given time
I check the gate to be sure it's barred tight
That no darkness can enter my paradise
But the fear is persistent
My heart's no longer at peace
And suddenly I'm paralyzed
Because the truth has struck me now
And I'm sickened to know that I'm the start
The darkness is here
It's already inside
Because I let it in my heart

Lonesome Grit

I'm just a lost soul searching for a better half
A present looking for a future better than the past
But I've been passed up so many times
Overlooked by everyone I've cared to find
And I'm starting to lose faith that there is anyone for me
These dilapidated chambers of my heart are so empty
Yet I keep my neck out on the line in hopes of some affection
Fearing always the chopping block beneath the guillotine of rejection
Its painful drop I've felt too often biting into me
Somehow intact, if not worse for wear, I'm left there where I bleed
Crimson spatters mingle with tears, but I power through the pain
It'll all be worth it, I tell myself, as I bear my heart again

Empathy

You say there's no way that I'd understand
That I can't comprehend
The loss that you feel
And the pain that you're in
That no number of miles
Walked in your shoes
Could transfuse an empathy
Or nurture a sympathy
Capable of miming the chaos
Under your skin
But I've been in the depths of your heart
A place of damp, cold, and dark
Where all but the brightest of lights
Just cast shadows that flicker and wriggle and writhe
Playing tricks on your eyes
As if there's something alive
In the desolate wasteland that's empty of life
Though you're all alone
And it felt just like home

Laugh

I think it must have been your laugh
That first caught me off guard
And hinted you were more than just
Another pretty girl
A lilting laugh
Sopranic tones
That danced within my head
Like beams of light
Within the dark
That I'd been living in
Enlightenment is a funny thing
Neither subtle nor outright
But relentless in the way it seems
To always set things right
Like silly thoughts of loneliness
Or thinking beauty is a long dead lie
When evidence suggests instead
That it is very much alive

Haleigh

This girl I met the other day while at the grocery store
I couldn't help but stare at her and wish I could see more
So I introduced myself to her hoping to learn her name
But found myself entranced by a face that put Venus herself to shame
Her eyes met mine, an ocean blue, liquid pools of azure fire
They drowned me in their depths then brought me back to life inspired
The palest skin, like winter white, yet full of warmth and vigor
Soft on the eyes, and perhaps the touch, no sign of roughness or rigor
Hungry for more, I baited her with humor, a hook of wit and guile
And found I'd hauled in so much more than just a pleasant smile
She let escape a little laugh, a sweet and silvery tone
That set her golden locks bouncing with a mind all of their own
And for a precious pearly moment I saw her lips gently part
Into a smile that could soften even the hardest of hearts
And somewhere inside me a warmth gently stirred
And my own smile widened, crude next to hers
Her name, she said, was Haleigh; I melted at the sound
And felt myself a pirate with this treasure that I'd found
But she's too rich for bandit loot, a jewel fit for the Louvre
No flaws in figure or character found, nor reason to improve
One day, I thought, I'll make her mine, that girl from the grocery store
And now it seems today's that day that I've been waiting for

Smile

When first I saw your siren smile
A sweet seduction of upturned lips
An entrancing beauty that so oft beguiled
To rocky shoals, doomed hearts like ships
I thought myself trapped in a dream
Though that was hardly right I knew
For even my most splendid thoughts
Could hardly craft the likes of you

Companionship

Within the chambers of my heart
You play a special role
Filling in the empty spaces of my mortal soul
How strange it feels now that you're here
Though often I have dreamed it so
For so long have I lived in half
At last I feel I'm whole

Hair

You may call your curls monstrous
Gorgon locks that jump and writhe
Almost as if they're conscious and alive
But I insist that they're just playful
A tasteful tease, a peek inside
Chaotic in their elegance
True beauty in the Maker's eye

Imagination

Imagine in a grain of sand
A whole world hidden from our eyes
Constant shifting of horizons
Pure creation in disguise
Now picture for me if you will
That swirling nexus rising up
And pouring out upon the surface
Like liquid flowing from a cup
Spreading out to other grains
Unshackling their sanity
Implanting in them their own source
Of pure creative energy
Now stand back, see what you've made
That grain of sand to you appears
A perfect copy of yourself
Reflected in a mirror

Heart

I think I love your heart the most
And since you gave a half to me
I understand now all too well
The patterns of its beat
Like the peaceful pulse of happiness
Tapping out in languid grace
In those moments of contented calm
While wrapped in my embrace
Or the war-drum rhythm: Forward March!
Pattering against your chest
Like a battlefield of butterflies
From vertigo induced by stress
Staccato strokes of nervousness
Steady throbs of poise
Hammer blows of rising rage
That cloud your ears with noise
The song of life plays to the beat
Performed within your breast
And I can't help but play along
Or at least attempt my best

Eyes

If you stare too long into the sun
Then you'll go blind they say
It's just too bright, that golden light
For any mortal gaze
But what if I were to tell you
That I know of not just one
But two great orbs, within them stored
Light brighter than the sun
And these two globes of sea blue hue
Won't blind a spellbound eye
But rather reveal the truth of sight
To a vision built on lies
Lies like beauty thought to be seen
In the mundane everyday
Now unveiled as dull and plain
Like a rainbow in shades of grey
For compared to the light and the life in those spheres
There's nothing quite the same
Because when I look into your eyes
The sun is a candle flame

Kiss

I love the way you kiss me
Not always with passion
But always with need
Soft, succulent lips often taking the lead
Whispered "I love yous" through scarcely locked lips
Ragged breaths coming in gasps and in sips
And my heartbeat is fluttering wild and free
Oh how I love how you kiss me

Solace

You always seem to lend an ear
When words spill from my troubled mind
Absorbing all my worries
And sounding off your own in kind
So never must I worry
About the words unsaid
Creeping up in later days
Compounded in our shuttered heads
Instead we lay them all to rest
And on that dirt construct
The foundation for a sturdy love
With no burdens to corrupt

First Kiss

Our lips draw closer together, a mere millimeter a minute
Such a small separation seems so vast, without limit
And luscious lips brush my rugged cheek again and again
Infinitesimal touches burn like fire on my skin
Minute position adjustments pull us closer together
And every second that spans seems like another forever
I can't imagine a moment more serene and pulse pounding
Like I'm floating away, but your perfect presence is grounding
Legs twined together haphazardly in sensual melding
Bodies merging, heat surging, tension grows overwhelming
Exhale in shuddering breaths, fear to shatter the silence
Hearts beat against each other's ribs with force verging on violence
And finally, climactically, tongues tasting one another
Lips brushing, blood rushing, each kissing the other
Emotions tumbling, I'm fumbling, such moments can't be defined
Our first together will forever be imprinted in my mind

No Strings Attached

Laugh it off, don't sweat it
Don't you get it
It depends on what you make it
As to how you'll take it
So just brush it away
Get on with your day
Leave it in the dust
Don't bust
Or make a scene
Keep your conscious clean
Don't dwell on wrongs
Just keep moving along
Living your life like your last day
Not letting strife get in your way
Heed this rhyme
And in time
You'll see
You'll be free

Combatting Calumny

The mascara runs down her face in black rivers
Her war paint in a battle for beauty
Where self-image is the enemy and conformity the prize
But she took a bullet cast from barbed words
And now she's dying inside
Bleeding inward where she'll drown in the insults of others
But mostly in the names she calls herself
Because she doesn't look like the impossibly thin dolls she used to play with
Or those women in the magazines she keeps on her shelf
She thinks the mirror is her nemesis
But it's really her eyes
Adding pounds and inches and lies
And measuring them all against a stigma of peer expectations
How can she know she's actually the subject of such adoration
That you watch her when she isn't looking
And see art in her figure
If you never say a word to counteract the far more vocal jibes, jests, and barely concealed sniggers
Your feelings aren't as obvious as you fear them to be
And what's to fear in taking note of natural beauty
A mumble of words uttered in a complimentary fashion
Could be the turning point in her battle for attraction
So be her battle cry and her armor and her sword
And who knows
You just might win the war

Transposition

What was it like to lose you?
It was like every laughably lighthearted
"I love you more"
Suddenly became a cold, bitter reality

The Architect

I wet the sands of time with my tears
And used our memories as buckets
To build a castle for my heart

Eighteen Years

I've lived and laughed and loved
And lost
I've risen and fallen, faltered and crossed
The line
I've trusted, lied, and suffered
Broken hearts
I've given and taken and weathered
And fallen apart
I've tried and failed, been accepted
And denied
I've cried and cried and cried
And died inside
I've believed, rejected, renounced
And embraced
I've stumbled, stood, fled, and faced
My fears
I've lived and lived and lived
And more
In eighteen years
It seems like life is anything but short

Infinite Inches

You say you want to just be friends
But you hold me like a lover
Shoulders, hips, and hands and foreheads
Pressed against each other
And yet when I lean in an inch
To close the gap between our lips
You turn your cheek and laugh it off
As if I didn't try to break the script
And when you leave all rosy glowing
You ask me why I never smile
And I can only shake my head
And fake one through my rising bile
Sometimes I want to push you down
And pin your arms back with my own
And kiss you there with all the passion
Of being alone
But I never give in to the urge
As strongly as it beckons me
Because I want you to want it too
I want for you to need
Not just friendship
Close yet distant
Not just hugs and almost more
I want for you to want to be my girl

Salt Wife

You push and you pull on my heart like the moon does the sea
And the tides rise up and they threaten to drown me
Any sane man would seek higher ground
But I cast myself back to the waters to which I'm bound
I beg you to wrap me in your seaweed embrace
To let me stroke the shells from your hair and the sand from your face
You take me by the heart and you take me by the hand
And we laugh and we frolic and we build castles in the sand
You know the life I yearn for and you give me just a taste
And then you lead me to the water and leave me under the waves
And I weep and I mourn and the ocean grows
And you push and you pull and the tide comes and the tide goes

Regrets

You're the best thing to happen to the world since sliced bread
And you're the best thing to happen to my life since anything
And I know you won't believe it
Hell I hardly do myself
But everything we've gone through only adds to our wealth
Of memories to draw from
When the water's getting rough
Life might rock the boat
But we'll be made of sterner stuff
Yeah life may hand you lemons
Or it may throw rocks instead
But you can use those rocks to build a wall
And shut out your regrets
And I only hope you don't count me as one

Inner Thoughts

When you look into my eyes
I try to fill them with my pain
But I only end up smiling
And kicking myself again
I break inside
I want to show you that I hurt
But I know I'm not the type
I don't want to live
But I'm too afraid to die
So I'll survive
I'm spending all my time
Musing on mistakes
They're bouncing in my head
And I can't seem to see straight
I'm losing my mind
I try to pull away
But the road just fades to black
I wander lost and lonely
Till I finally stumble back
Where light still shines
And I know it must be
Breaking your heart
That I can't hold myself together
I'm always falling apart
And blaming you
But I will try
To find my way
To stand without assistance
And live without you someday
Or die if I have to

Call to Glory

I want to live a love that ends in more than apathy
I want to love a life more bounteous than mine happens to be
I want to die a death more meaningful than disappearing
I want to leave behind a story that is worth the hearing
Yet here I stumble just another soul amongst the billions
No more important than the average worth of most civilians
I ride the fence between the sigmas on a normal curve
Convinced inside that I deserve to be an outlier
Where is the strife in life that unlocks my iceberg potential
The id inside of me fighting me to find adventure
I just want to find my purpose, I just need to find my destiny
I can't stand to be a character in someone else's history
So if you have a need I have the need to be the answer for it
To find the holy grail, to fill it up with life, and pour it
To be the aid, to be the hero, the protagonist in my own story
My ears are open and I'm hoping for the sounding of my call
to glory

Betwixt the Shadows and the Light

It's a beautiful day for misery
Scent of flowers on a summer breeze
The clouds are white, the grass is green, and I am blue
No chance of rain, but storm clouds break inside of me for you
Songbirds trill their happy tunes
Smiles catch and laughter blooms
And I prefer the company of doom and gloom
I used to join the joyous throng
High on life and glad it's long
But death has a way of sobering gaiety
And I did indeed die in a way when you left me
For no one would make the mistake of comparison
Between the person I was and the spectre I am
The sunlight is blinding to my blue heart and black mood
It's warmth incongruous to the cold I exude
And though dark my demeanor, I welcome the tranquility
Because it means not everyone shares these shadows with me
Yes, it's a beautiful day for misery

My Antidote

I used to think love was the symptom
And that you were the disease
I was happy to be infected
If my sickness could comfort me
But turns out you were just a vaccination
A little taste, just a little tease
Making me sick just to make me healthy
And give me an immunity
Now I pass through life unhindered
By the affliction of feelings I've come to crave
So I wound myself to invite infection
And beat my chest to feel an ache
But it does not come at my behest
No matter my appeals, no matter my pleas
It seems you've healed me of affection
And now I'm doomed to apathy

White Lie Love

You're like good graffiti on a cathedral
Still beautiful in your own way
But entirely out of place
We're both art on some level
And we once thought that made us the same
But that isn't the case
We're trying to interlock
Two pieces of different puzzles
And wearing our edges away
Pretending we fit
Because we almost look right
If we tilt our heads a certain way
We're doomed to imperfect metaphors
And terrible poetry
To try to explain our lot
Because you and me
We're almost meant to be
But we're not

Chapped

Try to smile through parched lips
Feel the blood trickle and the skin rip
So that every twitch of joy succeeding
Cracks old wounds, renews the bleeding
And that's just the start
Of the pain of a broken heart

Chasing Fireflies

The bulging rose hued sun slowly sunk behind the trees
The air perfumed by the scent of spring carried on a cozy breeze
From my vantage in the swaying grass beneath the arching boughs
I saw you barefoot dancing and I found my heart aroused
A knee length dress of baby blue swirled round your hips
And your golden hair, framed by navy skies, brought a smile to my lips
I looked up past the whispering leaves to the cloudless twilight sky
Where I saw the first stars twinkling and I breathed a contented sigh
A child-like gasp of pure delight drew my attention back to you
And I saw your face alight with joy, wide-eyed pools of sapphire blue
A brief little pool of yellow light lit up your growing grin
As a firefly flew lazily past the dimples on your chin
You danced across the blades of grass that tickled your tiny toes
Intent upon the lightning bug as it flashed about the grove
I smiled at the innocence and beauty of the chase
And in my chest affection bloomed as my heart began to race
I watched you as you left the grass and trod on grains of sand
Dancing at the water's edge, a firefly in your hand
You laced your fingers tightly, but it slipped right through the cracks
And a ringing laugh escaped your lips as once more you attacked
With outstretched arms you jumped and lunged upon the river side
And I watched with absolute horror as a nightmare unfolded before my eyes
Bare of any traction, I saw you sweet foot slip upon a moist rock
And as confusion filled your eyes, time shuddered to a stop
I felt my legs begin to move, but they struggled to comply

So long had I lain there staring at the sky
I followed your timeless journey as you plunged straight to the ground
A scream upon my lips that made no sound
Your golden head alighted upon a jagged stone
And the grove filled with sound of cracking bone
In an instant I was with you, water pulling at my knees
As I pulled you from the river's grasp with ease
Silence flooded in my ears as I shouted out your name
And you answered with nothing but the same
Then suddenly I saw the nightmare strand of diluted red
As a sickly stream of ruby blood pulsed from the back of your head
I looked into your perfect eyes of smiling sapphire blue
And there I watched them fade away as the life slipped out of you
The pulsing turned to a steady trickle in my shaking hand
And I screamed into the heavens; I could not understand
Tears ran down my face faster than the flowing of the river
And I swore my wracking sobs made the very leaves quiver
Then in a moment of cruel clarity my eyes grew wide with torment
As a little ball of yellow light interrupted my lament
The firefly flew on past and faded into the encroaching night
And I was left alone in a cruel world bereft of light
Two years and the present I sit upon the river side
Weeping into the same crystal waters in which you died
I do not weep at the memory of watching you pass away
But at the thought of never again watching you dance and play
At least when you perished you died as you lived beneath these twilight skies
Dancing barefoot by the river chasing fireflies

Bleeding Heart

I dipped the quill into my heart
And bled into the diary
Where my feelings formed the shape of words
That read like poetry

A Failed Attempt at Love

I tried to light a match
But it didn't burn
It snapped in half
And now it has no chance of catching
Without singing me

Evolution

When eternal darkness reigns supreme
When whispers come to you as screams
When pain no longer presents an obstacle
Then have the seeds of madness been sown

When you have a memory but not a mind
When you can see yet you are blind
When voices have replaced your friends
Then have the shoots of insanity taken root

When there is no line between right and wrong
When you speak in constant song
When your smiles turn into maniacal leers
Then have the stalks of dementia flourished

When you see happiness in a grain of sand
When you have crossed the sea and land
When thought comes to you without reflection
Then have the buds of genius bloomed

A Crack in the Pavement

A thousand seeds upon a gale
We'll only follow one
Some survive while others fail
The story has begun
A single seed is borne aloft
No different from the rest
But its trials will be far from soft
As it travels to the west
Over mountains, over seas
Over oceans, over trees
Crossing deserts choked with sand
Traversing icy no-man's land
It sails the skies unchained, unbound
Until the wind gives out
Then slowly spirals to the ground
Where metal mountains sprout
A concrete chasm marks its home
Beneath the tread of feet
It soon takes root in hidden loam
Immersed in summer heat
It won't be long until we see
Green shoots begin to show
So gather close and sit with me
So we can watch it grow
First appears a strong young stem
It's longer by the hour
Then sprout leaves both bright and thin
Like terraces to a tower
But on the top, what could it be
A silky blood-red bell
I guess we'll have to wait to see
For it to shed its shell
Now finally with climax come
Post adolescence looms
In dawn breaking Fate's harp thrums
And ruby blossoms bloom

Shooting Stars

On a dark night of clear skies
I asked if you'd like to take a walk
Though the grassy field behind our house
Where we could freely talk
But when you opened up your mouth
And filled your lungs with words and air
I bid you stop and stand in silence
For I'd just become aware
Of a presence in the darkness
In stark contrast with the night
I raised my rifle to my shoulder
And lined up my sights
You stood enraptured at my back
Awed at the accuracy required
As I put my finger to the trigger
Slowly squeezed and I fired

Baby you and I
We're shooting stars
Out of the sky
And if one falls at your feet
Will you pluck it from the earth
Hold it up for me to see
And find its glittering is worth
Less than the twinkle in your eye
Trapped like fireflies in jars
Baby you and I tonight
Are shooting stars

We watched it falling to the ground
A light trail bleeding in its wake
And you ran to try and catch it
Like a child chasing a snowflake
And I smiled when it landed
As you scooped it from the grass
And heard it tinkling as it died
A sound akin to breaking glass

I saw its fire flicker
Throwing shadows on your face
But even in its brilliance it couldn't quite replace
The fire in your eyes that warms my heart and lights my life
A shooting star in its own right

Baby you and I
We're shooting stars
Out of the sky
And if one falls at your feet
Will you pluck it from the earth
Hold it up for me to see
And find its glittering is worth
Less than the twinkle in your eye
Trapped like fireflies in jars
Baby you and I tonight
Are shooting stars

You cup your treasure to your chest
And I set my rifle in the dirt
Then you run and jump and hug me
Your star pressed between our shirts
All thoughts of talk are long forgotten
As we're lost in that embrace
Then I feel my pulse start quickening
As my heart begins to race
I look up in the sky
And see the countless stars still glowing
Reminders that tonight
Is not the last night I'll be knowing
Such happiness as ours
Can just be plucked right from the sky
Because tonight babe you and I
Are shooting stars

The Newborn Mother

Downy feather under head just one last chance to sleep
The baby cries, the mother sighs and fights the urge to weep
Softly singing lullabies, the baby starts to snore
The mother blinks, nods her head, and slumbers on the floor
Sunlight streaming through the blinds, the mornings come to pass
Footsteps muffled, she leaves her dorm then hurries off to class
Her roommate sends an urgent text halfway through a test
"The baby's sick, what should I do, you have to get here fast"
Pencil drops; she flees the room, and dashes to her dorm
The nurse is there, the baby's fine, his heads a little warm
The mother sobs, sinks to her knees, and looks up to the sky
She clasps her hands, she holds them high, and asks the great lord why
Why the baby, why right now, oh why did he pick her
No answers come, she bows her head, the world is a blur
She goes down, the ground comes up, a firm hand halts her fall
A warm embrace, an infant's face, the dark abyss withdraws
Another day, another night; the baby screams, the baby's quiet
Her grades still drop, her mother's right, her future doesn't look too bright
So she looks back at what went wrong to see what she can glean
And now she sees her problem was conceiving at sixteen

Yin

Stormy seas, sleepless nights
Whispered echoes, death, and life
Anger, sorrow, pain, and gloom
Misery its only boon
Softly creeping, makes no noise
Petrifying girls and boys
Always hiding in plain sight
Favoring darkness to the light
Greed and lust its only friend
It swift controls the minds of men
Needing, wanting, taking all
War, disease, and famine enthrall
Gruesome are its thoughts and actions
Torture, burn, and kill its factions
Stuff of nightmares making fear
Scream you would if made to hear
Voice of serpent in your mind
Hissing things most unkind
The demented in its shadow lay
Existing in both night and day
Pale wraith, foe of good
Shrouded in darkness, cloak, and hood
Everything you hate and fear
Builds its fortress higher still
Flesh its bread, and blood its wine
Feasts on sacrificial swine
Beelzebub, Antichrist, Devil
Lord of Flies, Lucifer, Yin, and Evil
Each a familiar title or name
Wrought from the pits of a hellish domain
Conceived in chaos, born of sin
A prince of destruction, a prince among men

Don't Feed the Fish

The big fish swim in the ocean
The big fish swim in sea
The little fish swim in the lakes and rivers
And the little fish swim with me
They swim beneath the surface
They swarm around the rocks
They glide across the sea floor
And they float beneath the docks
Some are long and skinny
Some are short and fat
Some are strange and some seem wrong
And some are just plain flat
They come with shells and pincers
They come with tails and fins
They come with teeth and whiskers
And some come dressed in pins
Some are orange and white
Some are black and gray
Some are brown, blue, green, or red
And some are clear as day
Some fish move
Some fish don't
Some fish swim
And some fish float
Some are huge
Some are small
Some are long
And some are tall
But it doesn't really matter
No matter what you wish
The rules will never change
Don't feed the fish

The Cobbler's Queen

A year ago I met a lass,
A beauty from the upper class
I watched her rather distantly
For just a lowly cobbler I be
But alas for I'm a guy,
I waved my hand and caught her eye

With but a look she stole my heart
And pierced it deep with Cupid's dart
Then she smiled and said hello,
Bowed her head and curtsied low
Desperate and without a plan
I bowed down and kissed her hand

Oh luscious lips and golden hair,
Rosy cheeks, soft skin so fair,
Trilling laugh, and emerald eyes,
She's Aphrodite in disguise
Tra la la and diddle dee
Oh she's the one, the one for me

Blushing bright she smiled at me
Then turned around and made to leave
Hoping she'd inquire the same
I found my voice and asked her name
She laughed and said "It's Madeline"
Then left without requesting mine

On the square I met that girl
Every day at half past four
We'd talk and laugh till it grew late
And with a kiss we'd end our date
So in love we fell each day
We both agreed to wed in May

Oh luscious lips and golden hair,
Rosy cheeks, soft skin so fair,
Trilling laugh, and emerald eyes,
She's Aphrodite in disguise
Tra la la and diddle dee
Oh she's the one, the one for me

Next day I met sweet Madeline
Surprised was I to find her crying
But when I asked what made her weep
She said she'd need a place to sleep
Her tears renewed, she'd say no more
And so we walked to my front door

With back straight and voice so neat
She told me I'd best take a seat
But 'fore I'd even grabbed a chair
She said she'd told of our affair
She'd told her dad, his voice was honed
With razor edge she'd been disowned

Oh luscious lips and golden hair,
Rosy cheeks, soft skin so fair,
Trilling laugh, and emerald eyes,
She's Aphrodite in disguise
Tra la la and diddle dee
Oh she's the one, the one for me

Alas that day for Madeline
For she had not but me and mine
With money tight and much to pay
We barely struggled through each day
A day, a week, a month passed by
And still was our world skewed awry

But to my shop a man did come
With gilded clothes and Midas' thumb
One hundred shoes he asked of me
And all of course top quality
Finally our luck had turned
We'd have the wedding that we'd yearned

Oh luscious lips and golden hair,
Rosy cheeks, soft skin so fair,
Trilling laugh, and emerald eyes,
She's Aphrodite in disguise
Tra la la and diddle dee
Oh she's the one, the one for me

One hundred shoes were we to make
A grueling task to undertake
For two more months we slaved away
We worked throughout the night and day
Though it took long the shoes were made
And oh our joy when we were paid

Since I met her it's been a year
And now our wedding day is here
When asked I proudly say, "I do"
For now I know it's really true
This cobbler's queen I take hold of
Is Madeline my one true love

A Doorway to Whatever

A doorway is from here to there
A doorway is from when to where
A doorway is from what to how
A doorway is from then to now
Sometimes open; sometimes closed
When one will open no one knows
From short on through to tall
From nothing through to all
From blindness through to sight
From darkness through to light
From outside through to in
From ape on through to men
From less on through to more
There will always be a door
But whether made from earth or stone
From rubber, liquid, flesh, or bone
Metal, plastic, wood, or glass
Imagination, air, or trash
A door alone to naught amounts
The opening is all that counts

The Music of the Chalkboard

Sometimes, sitting in Calculus
I miss the old days
Those pre-years where
When a problem is written
It sticks to simplicity
Now, as I'm called to the board
A dreaded symphony ensues
And my hands the conductor
A hundred marks here
Tip, tap, scritch, scratch
And I've composed the question
Another hundred there
Scritch, scratch, tippety, tap
And the orchestra plays an answer
Now, at the conclusion of my labors
I don't miss the old days so much
Because they didn't have it back then
Have what? You might ask
Why the music of the chalkboard of course

Crippled Dreams

I want to see the ocean
I want to see the sea
I want to see a rosebud
And I want to see a tree
I want to see a mountain
Or watch the rising sun
I want to see a diamond
And watch a wild horse run
I want to gaze at far horizons
And get lost among the stars
I want to trace the paths of raindrops
And see trains and planes and cars
I want to see the leaves of autumn
And the iris of an eye
I want to watch a heat wave simmer
And find shapes in cloudy skies
But for me it is impossible
To sate my starving mind
For though I wish it were not so
The truth is I am blind

What is Love?

Love makes you say things you never thought you would
Love makes you do things you never knew you could
Love gives you courage you never knew you had
Love makes you happy and love makes you sad
Love creates smiles and love creates tears
Love tears down walls and love conquers fears
Love is an arrow, a spear, and a dart
Love is a fire that burns in your heart
Love pierces hard and love pierces deep
Love controls waking and love invades sleep
Love is a message, a note, and a speech
Love can't be vocalized, written, or preached
Love is spontaneous and can't be refused
Love knows not singles for love counts in twos
Love is a blessing and love is a curse
Love is not prose; it knows only verse
Love has no boundaries and love has no walls
Love has its mountains and love, its pitfalls
Love knows not black, white, brown, yellow, nor pink
Love knows not tall, short, fat, skinny, or weak
So what is love and what does love do?
Well, love is me loving you

Window to the Soul

Upon the pane my breath awaits
A canvas for my heart to shape
Beyond the glass the world rolls by
Unseen before my listless eyes
And so your face devoid of flaws
My absentminded finger scrawls
First appear your sparkling eyes
Mirrors of distant sunset skies
While next take form soft curving ears
Subtle as a mother's tears
Then in my breath my fingers shape
The flawless sloping of your nape
And though through tears my eyes see naught
Your features still do my hands plot
First your hair as fine as lace
Then your nose and brows I trace
Chin, and cheeks, and surplus smile
Lashes, lids, and lips that rile
With salt-stained cheeks I do behold
A portrait framed in sunlit gold
A face I knew, the face I loved
Residing now so far above
Enticing clouds beyond my reach
A gap only my heart can breach
A death plot now my home from home
Such comfort in the broken loam
Beneath the land, above the sky
Your spirit rests for God knows why
So premature you part from me
The world, your friends, your family
But time goes on and so must I
Though you have passed you cannot die
Now traced in glass and trapped in me
You live within my memory

Window Facing West

I sit here on a Saturday alone like all the rest
On my second story balcony with window facing west
It's been six days since I saw you with your hair in braids and bows
With those eyes that light horizons and that smile that simply glows
Though it feels like its been ages I'll keep hoping for the best
On this second story balcony with window facing west

I stare out into the distance hoping I might catch a glance
Of the match to light the kindling of a fiery romance
But alas my search is fruitless for there's nothing there to see
So I turn my musings inward where I know you'll always be
There lies your image like a solstice to the pain within my breast
On this second story balcony with window facing west

Once more I turn my gaze upon the fast approaching night
As a thousand colors blossom from the slowly fading light
I start at every shadow thinking it just might be you
But succumb to further misery with your prolonged debut
I watch the shadows lengthen fearing what my eyes suggest
On this second story balcony with window facing west

As the dying sun and waking moonlight slowly intertwine
A silhouette approaches and the first stars start to shine
It climbs the eucalyptus and drops to my waiting arms
Where I embrace it with the fervor of a lover's secret charms
And we lay there deep into the night your head against my chest
On that second story balcony with window facing west

Children's Games

It's dark
The darkness is like a pressure on my mind
It's quiet
My heartbeats pound like hammer-blows on my eardrums
It's cold
My shallow breaths are all that warm me
My muscles are starting to ache
I shift my leaden feet and something brushes my arm
Something furry
I hear a sound
I feel a vibration
He's coming
He's getting closer
He knows where I am
I hear the rattling of metal
A light seeps across my feet
He's found me
Something slaps my wrist and I look up
I've lost
I step out of the coat closet
It's my turn to seek

Bloody Stripes

I march along as the trumpet sounds
Stopping here and there to fire off my rounds
The drum roll plays as my boots assault the soil
And the gun smoke's hot enough to make the oceans boil
I march along with a soldier to my right
While the one on my left isn't looking too bright
I can feel the blood a seepin' through my boots
Killing off the grass as it suffocates the roots
The stench of death perfumes the air
As we carry out the work that the Devil wouldn't dare
I watch the traitors come just a sea of roilin' gray
But we stack their bodies high enough to block the light of day
At last they've had enough and they turn around and run
So I shout hallelujah and I fire off my gun
We'd have chased em' straight to Richmond if McClellan weren't so slow
But instead we hold our ground and we let the bigots go
Well the drum roll settles and the smoke begins to yield
And the stars and stripes are flying on a bloody battlefield

Personal Apocalypse

I've always tried to take things slow
But there is just so much that I don't know
This world keeps spinning round and round
And I'd stand but I can't reach the ground
I can't see as far as tomorrow
I can barely make it through today
And I'd love to give voice to my sorrow
But I just can't find the words to say
I strain to hear the music ringing in my ears
But there's too much background static and I just can't hear
I'm like a frozen flame so full of energy
But I just can't seem to break free
I'm like an arm without a hand
And I'm digging a hole in dry sand
Though I try to hard to persevere
I'm drowning in my mounting fears
I see sand falling through the glass
An obstacle I cannot pass
Somebody help; I think I've lost my mind
And it's just so hard to find
Somebody help; I'm feeling so alone
And I just want to go home
Somebody help me please
There's something wrong with me
I'm like an ant in the falling rain
A child losing at their favorite game
I'm a hopeless wreck
In a world all my own
On an endless trek
With a destiny of threads un-sewn
My dreams lay shattered at my feet
With the promises I could not keep
But what can I do
I'm lost without you

I wake up every morning in an empty bed
With nothing but my sorrows and a storm above my head
Then I start to cry
And I don't know why
My world's an eternity of total eclipse
And I call it my personal apocalypse

The Curse of Love

I hang my head while my life falls apart
And a frozen grip grasps my shattered heart
I lose; Fate wins; once more I'm alone again
Oh what has happened to love

A girl walks by and my heart skips a beat
Then syncs its pulse to the tap of her feet
Cruel fate; why me; tell me this can't be
Oh not another false love

No not again; what's this feeling I feel
It must be a dream, but it's feeling so real
Make it stop; make it grow; this is a feeling I know
Oh could this really be love

No wait this must end; I can't do this again
But who am I kidding just look at me grin
No way; no how; I can't be doing this now
Oh but I think this is love

I follow her down to the end of the street
Where she turns around and our eyes meet
Can't hear; can't see; is it hot or is it just me
Oh this can only be love

She gasps, she swoons, and her knees give out
But I halt her fall with a whispered shout
I look at her; she smiles at me; and I melt beneath its potency
Alas once again I'm in love

With quivering eyes she proffers her lips
And I'm drawn into a prolonged kiss
No stop; not a chance; I don't do romance
Oh but I can't resist love

What a beauty she is, that girl in my arms
With an angelic physique and Satan's charms
What a catch; she's a keep; well at least for a week
Oh for the curse of love

Unrequited Love

When I first met you all alone
On an empty park bench like a royal throne
I stopped and stared because I knew
That one day I would be with you
No bells were ringing in my head
No shivers, chills, or hunches fed
And still I knew
I'd be with you
Without a word I took a seat
On fallen leaves and bird excrete
Hesitation didn't suit me then
And I know I'd do it all again
Well maybe never crossed my mind
Rejection lingered undefined
Because I knew
I'd be with you
A silent hour passed us by
And still I sat there by your side
Then finally you looked
And that was all it took
A thousand needles pierced my heart
And slowly my world fell apart
For now I knew
I'd never be with you
It felt so sure; it felt so right
A battle won without a fight
But it proved untrue
I'll never be with you
In silent pain I watched you leave
Condemned to love but not receive
In ignorance I climb the wall
But eventually I'm doomed to fall
From the gentle shove
Of unrequited love

Nature's Sympathy Pains

Nature is a fickle thing
It's never the same for long
And wherever you go it's always different from where you were before
Bubbling brooks, whistling winds,
Torrential rains, and stormy seas
I've often reflected on this curiosity and wondered at it
And I've reached a conclusion
Nature has emotions
Nature has moods
But what causes nature to be happy or sad?
Angry or calm?
Do Nature's emotions shape ours?
Do our emotions shape Nature's?
And if so then what is happening here?
Two months straight of mottled rain
One day blasted by searing heat
The next succumbed to biting cold
What do these extremes reflect?
Why is nature so frayed?
Are my emotions causing this?
But, oh, that's right
You broke my heart

Take Me Up From Reality

Well I look around and baby all I see
Are our people wading through a flood of poverty
And I can't help but choke up when they look at me
Those little faces staring out from piles of old debris
So take me up, to where the bloodstains fade
Where I don't have to think about the choices made
A place so far that I don't even care
About the strife or the hopelessness of our despair
Please take me up, where I can touch the stars
And forgot about the multitude of battle scars
The wounds will fade, but the memories stay
Reminders that assault my conscience everyday
Well I try to run and leave my aches behind
But every time I stop they're all that I can find
Oh take me up, and tell me what you see
When you look down upon the whole hypocrisy
Well I see blood and I see tears
And these are what they're calling our golden years
Brought on by fire, and forged by steel
This is the world; this is real

Drunken Romance

Every man in the bar just watches her pass
Then they turn their heads and they watch her ass
And nobody pays any attention to me
At the back of the room, an empty glass for company
A faulty hand swings out and makes a grab
Now he'd made a move he shouldn't have
I stand up on a swaying floor
While the hand moves up groping for more
A few lurching steps is all it takes
Before he finds my ring embedded in his face
The same ring that glints on her left hand
He should have noticed the wedding band
It doesn't matter; he'll no longer forget
But just for good measure I give him another hit
I take my seat and order another drink
The way things look it's gonna be a long night I think

Waking up to Paradise

Oh what a beautiful morning
Just look at that sun in the sky
If every morning were like this
I'd wish to never die
That's right I'd live forever
Just feeling the wind in my hair
Hearing the birds in the treetops
And never having a care
I'd climb the tallest mountains
And sail the seven seas
I'd march across the arctic waste
And swing through lofty trees
I'd wear the richest clothes
I'd drive the newest cars
I'd travel every country
I'd dine with movie stars
If every morning were like this
I'd live life to the full
I'd stare down death and danger
And I'd never play it cool
Oh if every morning were like this
I'd put the good life to shame
But alas this is impossible
For I've not a penny to my name

If Only If Only

If only if only the woodpecker sings
Over and over and over again
If only the worms didn't hide in their holes
If only the crisp morning air weren't so cold
But alas the poor woodpecker's cries go unheard
For who hears the chirrups of a disgruntled bird

If only if only the old soldier cried
Every time one of his partners died
If only the bullet hadn't flown so straight
If only he hadn't moved just too late
But alas no one sees the old veteran's tears
For he never leaves those battlefields

If only if only the fisherman yells
As the storm tears through his precious sails
If only he'd haul his nets up full
If only life weren't so cruel
But alas who heeds a salty sea dog
Making a living from a hollowed log

If only if only the child pouts
When the grown-ups fail to hear her out
If only she had the power to speak
If only her little voice weren't so weak
But of course who listens to an infant's cries
Brimming with answers to the world's lies

If only if only the world mourns
As it passes a history of divine scorn
If only its prayers didn't pass unheard
If only their loathing weren't so deserved
But there's no one to help and no one to aid
A world succumbed to an ignorant charade

The Underground

Born and raised in the squalor of a cardboard city
He fended for himself where he couldn't find pity
Surviving off the scraps of the underground
He was lower than the paws of a stray hound
Nothing he did ever amounted to much
And the world seemed to wilt wherever his feet touched
He passed his days in misery
Silently
Violently
Sometimes suicidally
He tried his hand at violence
But he could never silence
His frightened heart pounding at the final blow
Making every shot he fired shoot a little too low
So he fled back to debauchery
And begging for his money
But every coin he ever touched always turned to booze
Showing in the grip he was about to lose
Exponential regression
Homicidal obsession
Every passing second a painful life lesson
But he never learned, never turned his life around
Passing through life, eyes locked on the ground
Staggering pace
Never taking him any place
Eventually he'll fall
Harder than us all
Striking the ground with a muffled thud
Bottle rolling from a limp hand covered in mud
Glazed eyes focused on a cruel city
Car horns already playing his eulogy
He was never really anyone
Just another bastard son
Never missed, soon forgotten

Dismissed as misbegotten
The only mark he ever left was a bloodstain
Soon washed away in black rain
And high above the stars shine bright
Sweet light mocking a dark night
And the world keeps turning around
Heedless of the underground

I am King

I am the King, the overlord,
A dictator, the grand vindicator
I am a pillar of hope, a hero to my people
I am the top of the mountain, the one true steeple
When you're before me you best be on your knees
Your head to the ground, not making a sound
Except to say:

"You are the best; you are the greatest
The most courageous, and the absolute bravest
We yearn for your wisdom, and to your words we cling
We bow to your perfection for you are King"

When I pass you on the street you best avert your eyes
From my magnificence approaching undisguised
I've no need for a veil, or shady gauze
For my people love me and they love my cause
Wherever I travel, wherever I stay
There's only one thing they tell me, only one thing they say
They say:

"You are the best; you are the greatest
The most courageous, and the absolute bravest
We yearn for your wisdom, and to your words we cling
We bow to your perfection for you are King"

This is my turf, my land
Here you play by my rules or you die by my hand
I do what I want; I run the food chain
Why even the lion would soil his mane
Just to kiss the ground at my feet
And make my grand dominion complete
Because:

"I am the best; I am the greatest
The most courageous, and the absolute bravest
People yearn for my wisdom, and to my words they cling
They bow to my perfection for I am King"

Whatever I do, whatever I say
My people will back me all the way
To the ends of the earth, beyond the stars
Or else they shall wither behind steel bars
So what if they rot in poverty
Hey, at least they've got me
Which is fine because:

"I am the best; I am the greatest
The most courageous, and the absolute bravest
People yearn for my wisdom, and to my words they cling
They bow to my perfection for I am King"

Clouds

Sometimes while I'm walking I look up to the sky
And when I chance upon a cloud I begin to wonder why
Oh why the fluffy majesties never stoop to say hello
And if they did just what secrets might those giants know
Like stratus straddling far horizons must have heard a thousand tales
And windswept cirrus must have braved so many mighty gales
While cumulus with mountain's might towering high above the earth
Must horde a million memories within its hefty girth
And poor swollen nimbus weeping through the ages
Must have seen more sorrow than a Requiem's sad pages
Some people can find solace in clear blue skies
But all I find is loneliness and sunlight in my eyes
Those days I yearn for shadows to drift across the land
And fill my mind with questions I'll never understand
Clouds are like an art form found only in my mind
Which release me for a moment from the troubles of mankind
But I must continue walking and ignore my friends up high
Because reality is calling and I really must reply

Lost in Tranquility

I'm lost in the woods; trees all around
But for Mother Nature there's not a sound
No signs of habitation except for me
As far as I look sweet tranquility
Fresh air and clear skies
Nothing to hate or despise
Natural sustenance easy to find
Without the complications of mankind
For once I'm free
As far as I can see
Nothing to fear
In this frontier
Just living life
Free of strife
I'm lost in the woods; trees all around
And I don't want to be found

Shattered Skull and Broken Heart

Whatever I say, whatever I do
I just can't seem to make things right
And it doesn't matter that I love you
Because everything went wrong that night
I yelled at you, said things that I would never say
You slammed the door when I told you to go away
Now you're gone, but I'm still here
Heart verging on flat line
While I spend my nights awash in tears
Remembering the good times
The times when I loved you, the times when I needed you
The times I was happy that I got to live through
Now I'm looking back, heart broken in half
Wishing I were back when I still felt the urge to laugh
Where once we used to laugh at hundred different inside jokes
Now we spend every minute tearing at each other's throats
And now I see why they say
The heart is not a place to play
The pain it brings is incomprehensible
Because your heart is simply indispensable
Sleep, wake, call, wait
Is it too early or too late
I can't stand it anymore
I need our love restored
Ringing once, ringing twice
Will my apology suffice
It rings one more time
And then I hear your voice chime
I'm sorry babe if this is you
But we will never be together
I told you once that we are through
We just weren't meant for each other
Now you can spend your wasted life living alone

Don't even bother with a message after the tone
The phone drops from my hand and crashes on the floor
My heart can't take this pain anymore
I pull a pistol from the drawer beside my bed
And I set the greased muzzle against my head
A soft tone sounds beside my heel
And I to you with my last breath appeal
That whatever I say, whatever I do
I just can't seem to make things right
And it doesn't matter that I love you
So I will end my life tonight
I pull the trigger and a bullet bites my brain
But the darkness falls so slow that my body writhes in pain
And I hear a voice
As I start to fade
Sobbing at the choice
That I have made
And I wonder if you understand
That the bloodstain is not on my hands
It crashes on your tainted soul
Like waves upon a rocky shoal
You drove me to this precipice
With whispered words and loving lips
Then you shoved me with a cool dismiss
To fall into the black abyss
Now the light of life fades from my eyes
While a bloodstain marks my cruel demise
And all that's left when I depart
Is my shattered skull and broken heart
Forgive me
And maybe
Things won't be
So bad

Inaction

With my punch-dial telephone
And plush pleather couch-bed throne
I'm living like a bum in a lean-to shack
Sporting nothing but a tattered old gunny sack
I used to dine on platters of beaten gold
Consuming feasts at least twice what I could hold
I used to own this town; I used to rule that city
But that was before the damn committee
I was a good king
I always did the right thing
I treated my people fair
I was judicially square
I ruled this country peacefully
Patiently
A picture of nobility
With a hundred different suitors and would-be Queens
I had plenty of fun behind the scenes
Rolling in fame
I had no shame
I was at the peak of my life, the top of my game
Everybody loved me
I never had to worry
I guess that's why I didn't see
My coup d'etat destiny
I ruled in ignorance
Oblivious to pretense
While trusted advisors sharpened their knives
Power hungry fiends discontent with their lives
I was cast out, overthrown
Usurped of the royal throne
A treacherous committee was erected in my stead
And my people were convinced that I had died in my bed
Now military might became the law of the land
While fear gripped the people in its visceral hand

My reign is now a memory
While I reside in poverty
My glory days are well behind
A fact to which I am resigned
One day I'm sure
A hero will rise
And in gallant action secure
The committee's demise
I'll just sit back
I played my role
Let another rise
To seize control
The world turns
And the world burns
Good times end
And we all pretend
That things will be all right
Someone else will fight
You just have to trust
Leave it up to fate
And we fade to dust
While we sit and wait

It's Complicated

When you looked at me, what did you see,
Was I just something to be won?
Your one-night hoar, like an apple core,
To be tossed out when you're done?
And my broken heart, is it a piece of art,
Just a trophy on your wall?
Was my love so bad, was I just a fad,
Did I mean anything at all?
Every day and every night I strive to find the answers
But they flit around beyond my reach like ballerina dancers
I must admit that part of me is still in love with you
Despite all the things you've done and those that you still do
Something must be wrong with me if I can feel this way
My feelings are so jumbled and my heart's in disarray
If only there were someone who could make you disappear
Someone to mend the wounds you made and make my feelings clear
I need someone to love that will love me in return
But the only one I love is you and that's cause for concern

Long Distance Relationship

I kiss you goodbye
Saddened at your departure
But confident in the strength of our love
I tell myself we'll survive
Our bond is strong enough

Within a week I am lonely
Within a month I am lost
Within a year I have become a spectre
I pass the days in a daze
My eyes unfocused on the things that used to bring me happiness

While in my mind I walk amongst the hallowed halls of my memories
Our memories
But they have become worn and faded
Overuse has rendered them useless in sustaining me
My heart has grown callous to the pain

My only haven is found in the abyss of uneventful sleep
And with the rest comes the morning
And with it energy
But without you to ravish it upon it is useless
I cast it off

By the second year and your return I am a husk
You greet me with the fervor of my longing
But it is too late
I'm like a person starved too long
My body cannot support the sustenance thrust upon it

I am already dead

Allure

She turns off the television
And locks my gaze with pure precision
One crooked finger taunting me to follow

I comply without delay
Mesmerized by her hips sway
As she slowly saunters down the hall

Every piece of lingerie
Is begging me to come and play
With the figure sprawled upon the bed

As my garments hit the floor
I see the one that I adore
Watching every inch of me with hunger

She moans in exasperation
At my slight procrastination
As my fingers dance just out of reach

Finally I must relent
To her intoxicating scent
So I lean down and kiss her lips with passion

But the rest of her is beckoning
So I forget the day of reckoning
And I let my loving lips begin to wander

I feel my heartbeat start its climb
As our bodies intertwine
Expressing love the way that it was meant

Her panting breath assaults my ear
While her arms cling like a bandolier
For a moment time is frozen just for us

At last the waves of pleasure roll
And I relinquish all control
Confident the tide will take me home

I kiss her and I hold her tight
While the moon above heralds the night
Content to know that truly I'm in love

Black and Blue

Did you ever
Stop to consider
If I would be okay
And did you ever
Wonder whether
It was right to say
Those hurtful things you said to me
Are nothing but a memory
That keeps me on the ground where I belong
At least that's what you taught me to
Believe with every black and blue
Bruise you left on me; you were so strong
You were always quick to apologize
And that looked good through my black eyes
You didn't really mean it after all
You said I'd never hurt again
That this is where the pain would end
And for all your heartfelt lies I would fall
You hurt me all the time
But love's so hard to find
So I staunched my tears
And I hid my fears
And I said I didn't mind
The pain never made it past the skin
But your love resided deep within
My heart and that's what matters in the end
Your love was always black and blue
But that was all I ever knew
Another life I couldn't comprehend
So I took your love
And your abuse
I ignored each shove
And fell for each excuse

But every story has to end sometime
Someone had to pay for all your crimes
It's a shame you had to lose a wife
That this story ended with my life
So did you ever
Stop to consider
If I would be okay
When you hurt me that way
I guess that's what I get
For not wanting to admit
That I was loving you
In black and blue

Better?

Do you ever want
Do you ever need
Do you ever ask
Do you ever plead
Have you ever laughed
Have you ever cried
Have you ever lived
Then died
Do you ever lie awake in the middle of the night
Staring at a body bathed in pale moonlight
Has a smile ever kept the dark at bay
Have kind eyes outshone the light of day
Have you ever died inside
Your heart consumed by frost
Have you ever loved
Then lost
Have you ever spent a day just staring at the ceiling
Life devoid of purpose and heart devoid of feeling
Do you ever weep at memories
Knowing they are gone for good
And thinking if you could erase them all
You would
Have you trudged through life unnoticed
Not noticing in turn
Not caring if the world thrives
Or burns
Have you ever had your heart filled
Sloshing at the brim
Then found it empty, lacking feeling
And your future looking grim
If you have I have a question
That wisdom ignorance would call
Is it really better to have loved and lost
Than never to have loved at all

A Soldier's Motivation

Black cauldron bellows barrage my ears
Belching saltpeter smoke that taints the tears
The tears of corruption that pour down my face
Gouging deep trenches I will never erase
Washing off layers of dirt and mud
Exposing foreign crimson blood
Unearthly terrain cracks beneath my feet
The bones of the enemy, stripped of flesh, baring meat
Silvery stones burst at my heels
Spurring me forth to new and gruesome kills
The rifle in my hands no longer gleams in my eyes
It just reflects the faces of stolen lives
Every cracking shot resounding in my head
Echoing the screams of the newly dead
I trudge on in trance no longer asking why
So many good men must perish and die
Just to sate the revenge wrought on misplaced words
Spoken by old men with snakelike tongues and the brains of birds
The reasons hold no place in the chaos here
On this blood-soaked field of hate and fear
Only survival can conquer my mind
My body following suit as if blind
The job of a soldier is simple as can be
I just murder those labeled my enemy
It's kill or be killed on this battlefield
And only to victory or death shall I yield

Back to the Future

Please take me to the future
Where I don't have to think
About my missing link
So far away
I just want my breath to stop
For death to reap me like a crop
It really is the only way
Her death, came so fast, and tore my heart in two
I didn't even have time to cry
So now I've come to put my trust in you
To take me to the future
Where I can die
I don't want to suicide
And murder I will not abide
But I just can't live another day
Seeing life in shades of gray
I need to chase her fading light
Past the corridors of time
It's the only way to set things right
Let death's release be mine
Please take me to the future
To my end of days
So I can hold her in my arms
And hold her in my gaze
Please take me to the future
Please take me to my death
So I can reach my past
And take my first last breath
I must go back to the future
Where she waits for me
Outside the pearly gates
Soon myself her company

We Crusaders of Christendom

We rally to the call of the Vatican
We unite to fight the blight in the Levant
All Europe stands to strike at the Saracen
No white flag shall lure us to détente
We're falling down the rabbit hole pretending not to see
The shovel in our hand
While the fruits of our monstrosity
Ripen across the land
And the silver songs of Solomon fall deaf upon our ears
While sticks of sharpened steel assault the night
The holy ground stained black by crimson tears
A casualty deemed worthy for His fight
The ancestral sons of Abraham crumble into dust
To be stomped into clouds by steel shodden feet
While the daughters flesh sates our carnal lust
No nectar so sweet
The bodies lie in piles standing ten feet high
While blood collects in puddles and streams
The crows circle eagerly in the smoky sky
And the very air quivers with screams
Misty eyes populate the Bosporus
Taking us to Seljuk's mighty lair
While the crimson Croix across the strait escorts us
And we strut our march as a hero nom de guerre
Jerusalem's high walls mock our joy
An impenetrable fortress
But we are more than simple hoi polloi
And the city bows to our success
Through Fulcher's eyes we slaughter
Through our own we cleanse
But blood still runs like water
Whether it be foe's or friend's
At last we must ask the question
Was it worth it in the end
The thousands killed for obsession
With a deity's right to contend

Time Rains Eternal Pain

The drops of time are pattering on my head
Splashing my face with the past that I fear
And the future I dread
I cower at the memories that I see
Within each crystal drop
Mocking me
The specters of my childhood
The bane of my life
A memory of horror
An existence of strife
At every opportunity I hide
But it always finds me
No matter where I reside
Asleep or awake
Numb or aware
It knows where I am because it lives inside
Inside my head
Inside my heart
An experience who's amity I will never part
Every day is pain
Every night the same
My life a broken record
Repeating our game
Our little secret
Of flesh and lust
Innocence lost through misplaced trust
Bumps across my skin
As I relive it again
Every trailing touch
Every soothing word
Belying the thrusts
And the hurt they transferred
Paternal care
A nightmare

Sometimes I'd hear my flesh tear
And even though you're gone
I can never erase
The horrors you committed
A smile on your face
I live every day with the memories
While the drops of time rain from the sky
Knowing I can never live happily
Because memories never die

The Puppet King

I'm standing on my tower looking at the people
And wondering what they see in me
I'm just a boy, new to the world
And I don't know how to run a country
I don't know what to do, I don't know what to say
I don't know what's the right and what's the wrong way
I'm told how to look and I'm told how to act
I'm told what's fictitious and I'm told what's fact
I'm told what to think and what to believe
Who to ignore and who to receive
I'm told where to stay and where to go
I'm told what to forget and what to know
I'm a thoroughbred
Born to rule
I'm a figurehead
Just a tool
I have no opinion
So how can I rule men
I'm just a pawn in the game
Ruling on inherited fame
All the power in the world lies under my thumb
But Fate's threads are not mine to strum
I'm the marionette prince, I'm the puppet king
And I don't know much of anything
I'm just standing on my tower wondering
What my people see
In me

Schizophrenia

Opinions disputed
Emotions refuted
Asking softly of myself
Am I crazy
Voices fighting in my head
Mocking words I've never said
Telling me to run away
From myself
I'm chasing snowflakes through city streets
Creating wonders from cotton sheets
Finding joy where there is none to find
People say I have a problem
But they don't understand
That I'm just having fun
Enjoying life firsthand
They condemn my spontaneity
Say it's reckless and immature
But they don't have my vision
I don't need a cure
So I act like a child
Do you medicate them
Just for being wild
Or acting on a whim
I just have spirit
I don't need assistance
I am what I am
Isn't that God's insistence
My life is my own
So let me live
Because I've never quite known
Just how to forgive

No Fairytale

I'm not a damsel in distress, but
I must confess
When you swept me off my feet
My heart, it skipped a beat
You're not a hero
No shining armored knight
I don't need your help to set things right
But when you hold me
In a warm embrace
I can't stop the heat that lights my face
I'm a woman
I'm strong
But don't
Get me wrong
I may not
Stoop to much
But I
I melt in your touch
Take me by the hand
Take me from this tower
Show me the world
Show me power
Free me from this porcelain prison
But don't waste your breath on me
I'm not your little fragile flower
And I don't want your courtesy
I just want to live
I just want to love
So take my hand
Don't take my glove
I'm just a girl
Waiting for rescue
But I don't need a hero
I just need you

I'm tired of the fairytales
The princes, knights, and true love spells
I'm just a girl with one demand
I just want a man

The Burning of Ignorance

A boy once lived in the city of dreams
Head so full of wisdom it was bursting at the seams
He wanted to change the world, end life's sufferings
But there was too much hurt, too many screams
The screams of the dying, the screams of the dead
And a voice was building, resounding in his head
It said there must be something
Something you can do
Some way to help
And that was when he knew
He had a destiny, a calling, a path he had to tread
So he searched through all his knowledge, every book he ever read
Not yet a man, he began to formulate a plan
A plan so bold and daring others said you can't
But he said I can
He struggled for years living in penury
His life but a memory
A ghost of what it used to be
But he never looked back to reminisce
Self-pity was a distraction, a weakness to dismiss
He slaved away his youth, growing haggard and old
His bold mold of the future shining brighter than gold
Within the eyes of a dreamer in the city of dreams
He wasn't afraid to take his project to extremes
People called him crazy
Said he'd never change the game
But he said every pawn can be a queen
If there's a throne to reclaim
Time saw his bones grow brittle and weak
Death's grip already showing in the pallor of his cheek
But that was ok because his plan was complete
The nectar of his victory sweet
And with his final heartbeat he unleashed his feat

His life work printed and bound so neat
People stared in awe and confusion
At the leather-bound tome, the dreamer's conclusion
No words upon the face could identify its function
Just two strange lines in perpendicular conjunction
Fear of the unknown led to rash action
And the flames embraced the pages like some romantic attraction
Burning the hopes of the world and the hopes of the boy
A dreamer's lost cause for ignorance to destroy

Tease

Tell me girl, what should I do
When all I want in this world is you
You turn me away
Every day
My heart a board for this game you play
Why can't you understand
That all I want to do is hold your hand
Pull you close
Kiss your lips
Set my hands upon your hips
And dance the night away
But you always say
You tell me I'm not good enough
That you want a diamond in the rough
So I chip upon my soul
Looking for a sheen
And I polish up my smile until it gleams
But when you see me you shake your head
And say the words you know I dread
How we aren't meant to be
If only you could see
How much I need you
Want you
Love you
Why can't you
Love me in return
Why must you watch me burn
You give me just enough to make me stay
But what you hide and hint at drives me crazy
You're my Sunday confession
My not so secret obsession
Taunting me
Haunting me
Hurting me
Deeply
Why can't you love me like I do
You just love me loving you

Insignificant

We try to learn but all we find
Are questions burning in our minds
And everything we knew seems insignificant
Fire fire burning higher
Embers of the lands we've sired
And everywhere we've been seems insignificant
All we build just turns to dust
Stone is weathered, metal rusts
And everything we've made seems insignificant
Crows are calling, bombs are falling
Death toll count is sheer appalling
And all for which we've fought seems insignificant
We ask for divine assistance
Questioning our own existence
And everything we are seems insignificant
Laying on our death bed our passing is ignored
And time without our presence is easily restored
And everything we've done is insignificant

The Friendship

We became best friends in second grade
You were the only one not afraid
To introduce yourself to the new kid on the block
Now turn the clock
We spent a few years getting into trouble
Just a couple kids outside the social bubble
Time ticks by
Child habits die
Middle school arrives
And our friendship thrives
But time moves on
And so do we
It was my freshmen year
I saw you differently
I caught myself watching you leave
The sway of your hips mesmerizing
But we were just good friends
So I lied to myself
I bundled up my feelings
Hid them high on the shelf
But as the years moved by
I couldn't deny
The way your curves drew my eye
I'd make you laugh just to see your smile
Every little second together worthwhile
I found myself falling asleep
Staring at a picture of you
The way I felt just didn't make sense
It defied what I thought I knew
We were just friends in your eyes
But my heart said otherwise
So I loved you secretly
Pretending you couldn't see
The way I stared

The way I cared
The way I wanted what couldn't be
Then one day in our senior year
I couldn't take it anymore
All inhibition disappeared
I had feelings I just couldn't ignore
I walked you home from school
But I didn't leave you at the door
I had words that I had to say
But all is fair in love and war
You saw the three words hanging in my eyes
And put a finger to my lips
Then set your arms around my neck
And let my hands fall to your hips
And the words were left unsaid
Floating in my head
But you heard them all the same
No shame
That kiss
Just bliss
We became best friends in second grade
And in a decade
The friendship ends
And the love begins

Running From Today

You're running to the edge
The edge of the dawn
The dawning of a new day
But horizons are forever
So you never reach your destination
You just run until your feet grow sore
And you search for
A target to vent your frustration
What you do
What you see
Filed into memory
A dog upon your weary heels
You kick it but it never yields
Life is just a shadow
Overshadowed
By the shadow of the sun
You can hide but it will find you
And remind you
Of the reasons that you run
Your mistakes
Join to make
Make the person that you are
And you hide them
Override them
And dash for the morning star
Every day is a new day
Every day is the same
And only you can ever change your name
So you run
And you run
To save yourself
From everyone
Accusing eyes
Seek your demise

Because they know
What you have done
You are running to the edge
The edge of the dawn
The dawning of a new day
And if you ever reach tomorrow
Fleeing sorrow
Who's to say
You can't stay

Caroline

There is a place that matters not with little much to see
But in this place you'll find a girl of unmatched majesty
A twilight princess in her right, with light that shames the sun
Her beauty is unmatched, supreme, and paralleled by none
With locks of hair rich golden brown, like freshly risen bread
Caressing high held shoulders as they dance around her head
Her eyes are irises of sapphire inset in whites of pearl
Locking deep within them bright stars that flash and swirl
Her smile could light horizons, and guide ships safely home
As they brave the seas to seek her heart, the Cleopatra to
their Rome
Never did you hear a sound as sweet as is her laugh
Her sadness brings about more tears than any epitaph
The world revolves around her, begging to be seen
Knowing it can't have her and glowing envy green
Her touch is like a little shock, tingling on your skin
A feeling you cannot explain, but wish to feel again
Perfection is too small a word to possibly define
The everything that is the girl I know as Caroline

Stone-heart

I know you understand the concept of forgive and forget
Don't tell me you're not ready to come back yet
I'll show you what it means to leave me
Discreetly
Completely
Six feet of dirt excavated so neatly
You tell me you don't love me anymore
You slam the door
Leave my heart bleeding on the floor
And there's nothing left inside of me but anger and hate
Baby it's too late
My wrath is released, my mood sour
My balled fist clenched with restrained power
Cold rain lashes against the window sill
Time stands still
And my fist strikes the tense glass
A momentary impasse
Then I hear the shatter
But it doesn't matter
Spider web cracks shoot out from bloodied knuckles
The rain chuckles
And I try to see through my tears
But all I can see are three lost years
Then I see your face in the cracks on a window pane
And I know I've got nothing to lose and everything to gain
Why did I let you go
Baby I hope you know
That nothing I did was ever meant to hurt you
And I apologize for everything I put you through
All the emotions that I felt, but never wanted you to see
I put them in a bottle, hid them deep down inside of me
But eventually
The top popped
My heart stopped

And the smile on my face was Photoshopped
I wore you down with my battered pride
I said you'd given up, but I know how hard you tried
I'm the only one to blame for the problems that I face
And now I see that you're my saving grace
My love for you has never faltered
The way I show it has just been altered
Baby I promise things will change
I know my limits, I know my range
I know I've said it before, but I mean it this time
I've already paid for my crime
Baby don't you see
I already hurt you so please don't hurt me
Two wrongs don't make a right
Forget this night
Forget this fight
Baby come back
Your job is to defend, not attack
All I want is for us to be together
Two birds of a feather
Through the good and the bad weather
I'll do whatever it takes
I know I made mistakes
I didn't know the stakes
Now I do
The price is you
Baby I'm going crazy
Is it even possible to start over new
Please won't you listen to reason
I'm opening up my heart
These tears I'm blaming on the season
But I'm tearing myself apart
Is the pleasure even worth the pain
Is the loss really worth the gain
Everything I do for you
I manage to screw up somehow

It doesn't even matter if it's true
It's too late now
I had my second chance
I blew it
I put pleasure before romance
We both knew it
Now you're gone; and I'm alone
With a broken heart that's turned to stone

Try, Try Again

When I was thirty years old I got fed up with my life
I had a mediocre job, no kids, and no wife
So I gathered my belongings and tied them in a sack
Waved farewell to my hometown, said I don't know when I'll be back
Now fifteen years is a long time to run
Every day following the rising and the falling of the sun
It took me a long long time traveling this way
Before I realized I was just treading the same path every day
I trudged back home hanging my head in shame
Knowing my lackluster life would always be the same
But my spirit was always restless and yearning for a challenge
So once again I left my hometown and I headed for the Fringe
Now the Fringe was a mountain range of horror and awe
With peaks so high that snowcaps never felt the springtime thaw
But I was determined that I'd climb them to the top
So I put my arms in motion and vowed I wouldn't stop
Now I was true to my word and I climbed for days and weeks
But every time I looked I was no closer to the peaks
By the time a month had passed I was too weary to continue
So I dropped to the ground knowing I was through
It was then I saw the problem that had blocked my climbing higher
For I had climbed the mountain sideways rather than scaling up the spire
So I headed home again defeated and sore
Knowing I'd remain a failure forevermore
But Fate's will can never be denied
And new paths of my destiny could not remain untried
So I took up a tool and headed off into the night
Guided by nothing but pale starlight

I walked until the sun rose swollen and round
Then I took up my tool and broke the ground
I dug and dug grain by grain
I dug in the sun and I dug in the rain
I dug for years and decades more
I dug until my body grew sore
And finally as my heart grew still
I had a six foot hole for me to fill
Now some have called me a fool and a loon
For digging my grave with a table spoon
But at least when at first I did not succeed I tried again
And I managed to complete my task in the end

End of the World

A dry wind stirs the dust of empty streets
While high above a gray sky weeps
For the destruction all around
Where there's no life to be found
A sad day for humanity, another day in time
An apt sentence for the crime
This is the end of the world
This is where the story ends
No glory to be had
As a silent sun descends
Crumbled monuments cast shadows on burnt and twisted trees
And the odor of death perfumes the breeze
A thousand fires flicker under shrouded stars
And the roads are filled with the burned out husks of ancient cars
Twisted spires of metal brush the bellies of ash clouds
And a rotten wind whips the garbage of the past into crowds
This is the end of the world
This is how things settle down
The result of discordance
And the battle for a crown
Old bones crumble into dust when kissed by wispy wind
The remnants of a people who tried to pretend
That their power was untouchable, immune to time and trial
A people in denial
They have paid for their folly with eradication
But the scars they left are nothing short of desecration
Even boundless time gives vent to its frustration
And allows itself to crack a silent smile
This is the end of the world
A beginning and an end
And things are looking better
When man cannot distend

This is the end of the world
This is where our faults commune
This is the end of the world
And this is soon

The Last Goodbye

One day I met the world with gasping cries
Grasping fingers with strength incongruous to my size
And a woman's voice caressed my little ears
While cool lips brushed my head through loving tears
Then I said

This is goodbye to certainty
This is farewell to pre
This is so long to obscurity
And this is hello to me

One day I found my memories rejoicing in my mind
Reminiscing in nostalgia of the years I'd left behind
Of the constant daily struggle and trying to survive
The learning of all deemed essential for me to thrive
Then I said

This is goodbye to childhood
This is farewell to youth
This is so long to bad and good
And this is hello to truth

One day I met a girl with a broken heart
Drowning in her tears as her world fell apart
I pieced her back together with a warm embrace
I put a ring on her finger and a smile on her face
Then I said

This is goodbye to solitude
This is farewell to blue
This is so long to getting screwed
And this is hello to you

One day I had a night of pleasure and joy

Nine months later I had a small baby boy
I watched as you kissed him on the head
And witnessed the Fates weave a brand new thread
Then I said

This is goodbye to quiet nights
This is farewell to two
This is so long to living cheap
And this is hello to new

One day you died and left the Earth
While I remained devoid of worth
And I reflected on my life
And wept for the memories of you, my wife
Then I said

This is goodbye to happy days
This is farewell to fun
This is so long to love's soft haze
And this is hello to one

One day I breathed my very last breath
Then passed without feeling or care into death
In truth I had died those long years ago
When with the death of my wife my fire ceased to glow
And I said

This is the end of living
This is where I die
This is the taking after giving
And this is the last goodbye

Conformity

One day I was a boy and I loved to write
I was a poet and with my words I'd fight the good fight
I had the vision and I had the sight
But not everything turned out as it might
People I loved set another path for my feet
And I was introduced to the people I needed to meet
My tempo begged to make its own beat
But there was too much resistance and it was simple to defeat
So I conformed to the structure of the social frame
I learned to play the social game
And my days blurred and became the same
My writing transgressed to the signing of my name
And I tried to salvage what I could as I burned in shame
I bundled up my hopes and I bundled up my dreams
I wove them in a tapestry but it started fraying at the seams
So I stashed it in the attic far away from the sun's rays and the moon's beams
To be opened again one day but not everything is as it seems
And I fell into the same daily routines
I ignored my destiny and shunned my fate
I had no worries except the money in my wallet and the food on my plate
And soon enough it was too late
I had spent too many years in wait
I would always be mediocre, I could never be great
And late at night I'd reminisce the time
So long ago when all I wanted to do was write and rhyme
I didn't care whether I had a fortune or a dime
I was living and giving and that was just fine
And now when my feeble hands grip a pen in hope
No words flow before my cerebral grope
I'm drowning in a sea and just out of reach of the lifesaving rope

I walked off my peak and I'm too old to climb back up the slope
My time is over and done
I've lost where I could have won
I walked when I could have run
And my only relief is the barrel of a gun
I put the muzzle against my time wrought temple
And tears blur my eyes that I find it so simple
I lived a life of regret
Of the things I didn't do and the things I didn't get
Now my path is set
A flash of pain in my head
My tears turn red
And I'm dead

The Moon's Advice

One day the moon looked at me and said,
"Why do you weep?"
And I said to the moon,
"Because my love will not keep."
And the moon replied,
"Then why this love do you seek?"
A tear kissed my cheek and I said,
"Because mother moon, my life is so bleak"
I watched the moon sigh and turn away
And then I heard her softly say,
"Once I loved as you and more
But love is little but a whore.
So much did I love the sky,
Though at the time I knew not why,
I asked her if she loved me too,
But she said not with my pale hue.
She called me dull and turned away
Then kissed the sun and they made day.
I shed great tears and dimmed my light
And so made the oceans and the night.
So my child don't you see?
Love is not for you or me."
Then I said to the moon,
"So mother moon I must ask why?
Why have you never left the sky?"
The moon's pale gaze returned to me
"Why, my child don't you see?
The sun and sky may share a life
But the sky has always been my wife.
Though I may never share her heart
Her presence I can never part.
So seek your love if you must
But never in love should you trust."

Clock

Life is a clock
Tick
Tock
Every beat of the heart is a turn of the hand
Another grain of sand
Striking the bottom of the glass
Let's watch life pass
Little but a child
Always running wild
Driving everyone he knows insane
Little does he care
About the world's affairs
Life to him is nothing but a game
Add some years
Smoke and mirrors
Now he has grown into a teen
Body strong
Life seems long
Horrors of the world as yet unseen
Blink of the eye
Time flies by
Society welcomes a new man
Everyday rehearsed
Family comes first
Working just as hard as he can
Sleep away
Many days
Hale a man of wit and wizened years
On death's door
Memory poor
Life to him a vintage souvenir
Life is a clock
Tick
Tock
Frozen for a moment with a smile
So make sure every moment's worthwhile

Shortchanged

Well I have lived and I have loved and through it all I wondered how
How I could have survived the way I lived before and now
So lonely, no one here to hold me in their arms and say
Just how much they love me and they don't want me to go away
Away
Now every time I turn around my memories are all I see
Hauntingly they're taunting me with all the things that used to be
And now
I'm picking up the pieces of my broken heart and wishing that I'd never felt those feelings that I felt
Skin so soft and hands so warm I feel as if I just might melt
I melt
But I coalesced into a ball of pain and grief and through it all I continued to wonder how
How can I live now
Looking to the future I see everything I want to see,
Everything I want to be
Everything I want to do,
Everything except you
So baby
Please tell me
Why did you have to die
And leave me here to cry
I thought that the world was my oyster
But I found that it is just the cloistered
Hall of grief
Hall of pain
Hall of you calling my name
Every night I stain my sheets with another rush of tears
Remembering the years
And living my worst fears

I'm feeling so alone
Vibrations in my bones
Wracking sobs that tell me things have changed
Fate has left me shortchanged

Epiphany

I walk across an endless field of broken hearts
I can't tell where the pain ends or where it starts
I'm watching sorrow swim in a river of tears
Hopes and dreams drowning in worries and fears
And the worst part is realizing I'm not alone
It seems the whole world calls this place home
I see more frowns than smiles
I hear more sobs than laughs
Happiness defiles
This land of epitaphs
Everyone seems lost
Wounds engraved, scars embossed
And I'm just one more soul
Wandering in this hell hole
Wondering at my purpose
Not sure what I should do
Wishing someone would help us
To start over new
And finally realizing the only thing that's true
If you want life to change, it's up to you

The Day the Towers Fell

The world seems to whisper as time shudders to a halt
Action distant and undefined as people try to find the fault
Confusion on the faces of the children, shock on those of the men
No one quite believing it could be happening to them
A smoke cloud in the distance seen by all
None quite sure yet what it signifies as they watch the tower fall
Rumors flying faster than the ashes from the fires
Accusations on the T.V.'s and hysteria on the wires
Screaming sirens silenced and the country sees the worst
As the second tower kneels to kiss the steel bones of the first
Heroes wading through the ashes of the victims like the blind
Rooting through the rubble for any trace of survivors they can find
Little white stars gleaming as they cling to tattered stripes
Rising from the jumbled pile of concrete and twisted pipes
A hopeful little beacon choked by gray-black dust
Barely noticed through the smoke smeared tears that flow for the unjust
A dry wind warmed by hate and fire sighs through empty streets
As a country sunk into despair silently weeps
A day of utter sorrow and a sorry woeful tale
A tragedy we'll not soon forget the day the towers fell

It Starts With You

Quick, raise your hand if you ever thought you were in love
Only to discover it was just a fantasy you were dreaming of
And then reality hits you in the most literal sense
The affections of your once upon a time fairytale prince
Letting you know just how much he cares and how much he doesn't want you to leave
And you're screaming at him to back up, give you some space so you can breathe
Then he slaps you across the face, tells you've got a choice
He says either next time it will be his fist or you'd better lower your voice
Because there's a child in the next room trying to sleep
Except at that moment that child is wide awake listening and trying not to weep
As he hears you, his mother, raging at his dad
Saying you're going to call the cops if he hits you again and you know it's kind of sad
Because you never even stop to think that maybe this isn't the way love is supposed to be
You just assume that everyone goes through this; it's the price of family
Shhh, now whisper as you slumber in your bed
Bruises on your body and bruises in your head
His gun against your temple, you're knife against his throat
Bloodstains on the pillow like a sappy love note
It's all you've ever known; you can't imagine more
The world is no better beyond your front door
And the sad part is you're kind of right
This world sees so little light
It seems to happen everywhere
Over here and over there
An all-consuming darkness swallowing our souls
Spreading animosity through the minds that it controls
And who can hope to combat something so beyond our scope

Of reasoning that we have almost lost all of hope
Well I'm here to let you know that if you can no longer tolerate
The endless hurt and the mindless hate
And all you want to do is start over new
Then it's time to realize that it starts with you

Pandora's Wall

A long long time ago
I laid down a brick
Spread the mortar on thick
And divided myself into two
I just didn't know what else to do
Because you see
For one such as me
This world is a dangerous place
Peopled by a dangerous race
And I needed to protect my heart
So I split it apart with a wall
Strong and tall and unbreakable
But unshakeable as I thought my protection
Its design had one little imperfection
And despite all that it can do
I forgot to take into account
A certain amount of you
It was such a long long time ago
I built that wall
So, after all that time I forgot
Whether it was still there or not
And so when our eyes first locked
And time stopped
I was quite surprised
To see in your eyes
Not the reflection of my star-struck face
But rather the base of a bulwark of brick
And I felt rather sick
As I realized that somewhere within my heart
Deep down inside
Resides a divide
Keeping myself apart
Instead of keeping myself alive
An impenetrable wall

Separating all
And whatever I do
I can't seem to break through
I just want to be free
For on one side is me
And on the other is you
But try as I might
I could not right the wrong I had done
When one day long ago I divided my soul
Into two parts of a whole
Locking my heart in a tomb
Without enough room for two
Forever leaving me without you
So a warning to all
Who might build their own wall
Don't

The Cycle

Here I am late at night, sitting in our room
Wondering if it's too early to assume
That if I call you'll take me back
Let you switch from the defense to the attack
After all it was me who broke up with you
I told you we were finally through
I was just so tired of the alcohol and the drug abuse
The misuse
So I had to do something to you before you did something to me
Don't you see
Because between the two of us we've got a job to do
A three year-old daughter depending on me and you
To set our problems aside
To coincide
Because these barriers between us are just too much for her to take
She's fragile and we need to be careful that she doesn't break
Like it breaks my heart when she cries
See the tears gleaming in her eyes
Those beautiful blues
The one thing I just couldn't bear to lose

This is life as we make it
Leave it or take it
But never mistake it
For anything but what you've got

So here I am reminiscing about the happy past we had
And wondering if the future will be anything but sad
When suddenly my thoughts are ripped violently apart
By a banging on the front door and a scream that pierces my stony heart
And I run to the window time passing as if in a dream

My face a mask of horror as I hear another scream
Red taillights burn an image in my head
Of my beautiful daughter stolen straight from her bed
With her beautiful face pressed against the glass
Screaming for her daddy as her drunken mother puts her foot to the gas
Then time resumes at its usual pace
And I'm already flying down the stairs sorrow evident on my face
By the time I reach my car I already know it's too late
As you disappear around the corner streetlights reflecting off your license plate
I search for two hours in vain
Tears pouring harder than the pouring rain
And I've already called you six times with no reply
But I have to give it another try
You don't answer and I have no choice but to return
And let the fever of worry burn
As I pass a sleepless night unsure what to do
Cursing my foolishness and cursing you

This is life as we make it
Leave it or take it
But never mistake it
For anything but what you've got

Early in the morning, a table set for two
I'm eating alone and watching the news
It's gonna be a fine day, sunny skies
Incongruous to the chaos thick behind my eyes
Traffic is backed up on fifty-three
An overturned big rig and a crushed Camry LE
Seems the driver of the Camry had a BAC
Just a little over point two three
She's doing just fine, not even a broken bone
Problem was that she wasn't alone

White milk a growing puddle on the floor
I'm already out the front door
Half an hour later I'm on my knees
Looking at a little bundle on a stretcher yelling please, no, please
I'm shaking my fist at the sky
Asking a God I don't believe in why
How could you take my beautiful girl
How could you snuff out the brightest light in this cold dark world
Strong hands on my shoulders pulling me away
Telling me it's going to be okay
And that's when I see you, a tear in your eye
As if you have the right to cry

This is life as we make it
Leave it or take it
But never mistake it
For anything but what you've got

Two years later, you've got prison for life
I'm short a daughter and rid of a wife
I try to move on, stay positive
But I lack the prerogative
I just can't forget those beautiful blues
And how right they are to accuse
After all it was me who broke up with you
I told you we were through
And now I pay for my sins
Here my torture begins
A life without living
The ultimate giving
Now I'm a ghost, a shade
A cur to degrade
If you could see me now, if only you knew
I'm inheriting the very problems for which I cursed you

A hypocrite living on a drink and a fix
A needle and pack of six
But nothing can wash out the images I see
Of a beautiful little girl smiling between you and me
And nothing can stop the flow of tears
Too many to count through these miserable years

This is life as we make it
Leave it or take it
But never mistake it
For anything but what you've got

Plea

You say some things aren't meant to be
But open your eyes and you'll see
The twisting strands of Destiny
Striving to merge desperately
The silk swathe of you
With the frayed patch of me

Not all you see is as it seems
Gold glitters but silver gleams
Your shattered wishes and broken dreams
Shrieking tears and muffled screams
May seem like all you know
But they're only the tattered seams

So when you say our love won't last
Comparing us to a poisoned past
Let all expectations be surpassed
And know the future's die's been cast
Quickly now prepare yourself
For watch as it approaches fast

Let inhibitions fall away
Like the night before the day
I bare my heart for your display
Please listen to the words I say
Whether they bring you joy
Or bring me dismay

It longs for you like braying hounds
More devout than hallowed grounds
Hear it now as it sounds
On the door of your heart it pounds
My love for you cannot be restrained
For it knows no bounds

Drama

Drama, drama, drama
Don't you wanna just be happy
I know ex-act-ly what you need
You need my arms around your shoulders
A whisper in your ear
Telling you that it will be alright
You don't have to fight it anymore

Oh drama, drama, drama
Don't you wanna just feel better
How could you let her
Claw her way into your heart
Tear your feelings apart
And leave you to die
Now I'm here and you don't have to cry anymore

Well I've got a lot of love to give
And I would give anything to live my life with you
This time I'm meaning to stay
You won't be pushing me away the way you do

So take my hand, and I'll take your heart
And we'll pull this world apart at the seams
I know you think that love is mad
But it's really not so bad as it seems

Oh drama, drama, drama
Don't you wanna just rest easy
Let's find a breezy spot upon the beach
And we'll each find peace as time slips away
Give in to love and face the pain another day

Remembering the Future

Everything I do
Comes down to this
A single kiss
Between me and you
I wish it didn't hurt so much
The memory
Of that touch
That only ever happened in my head
Just a dream
A wistful thought
It would seem
I'll know it not
Cursed to live in loneliness instead
Sometimes I catch myself licking my lips
Beads of moisture growing
A leaky faucet, my eye drips
Loss like water flowing
Will the future ever hold
Me holding onto you
And just what do I do
If the glitter is not gold
But rather just the tears within my eyes
And how can I expect to live
In the shadow of a kiss
I can only reminisce
What I would give
To experience the love that life denies

Love Triangle

I need to give words to my sorrow so I pick up my leaden pen
Only to sit in silence before setting it down again
For how can I find words to tell you what you already know
After all you share my grief within this tale of woe
A tale about two lovers, those lovers, me and you
Doomed to crave what cannot be no matter what they do
Because there is another lover within this geometry
A man who both binds and divides the feelings between you and me
For he is the man of fortune, who found a queen to share his throne
While I remain ostracized, unrecognized, alone
He is the one who holds your heart in view for all to see
While I lust from the shadows, loving secretly
My heart consumed by envy when I watch him take your hand
Hatred deep within me that I cannot understand
Because, the worst part of it all, he is a friend of mine
A close friend whose view of me is nothing but benign
Why did this have to happen, why did he find you first
And would he feel the same as me were our positions reversed
I just can't stand this anymore; I don't know what to do
Because all I want in all the world is to go on loving you
Lose a friend, lose your love, lose them both in time
How can I pick between the two when the decision's not even mine
I do not envy what you face, though I pity me as well
For there can be no happy ending to this woeful tale

Rejection

I've got a couple things to get off my chest, just a few things I need you to hear
So maybe you could lend an ear to these words I have to say
Even if you just ball them up and throw them away
Because the truth is I've got a lot of things bouncing around in my mind
So many emotions in jumbled commotion that the truth has become impossible to find
Basically I think it's time I let you know exactly how I feel
Because the cliché's got it wrong, some wounds never heal
And it's time that I removed this shady veil
You see I love you and I think I always will
Now I know you've already made your decision
And I'm not here to try and bring the problem back to the table for revision
But I have an irrevocable need to set some things straight
Right now I'm like a starving man pushing his food around his plate
And I'm not trying to point the finger
Lollygag, lurk, or linger
On the things you say and things you do
After all I'm just as guilty as you
But what I can't seem to understand
Is how you can take his heart and hand
Then tell me that you love me all the same
But who am I to say since I'm to blame
There were so many things we could've been, should've been, could still be
If only you were leaving him, instead of leaving me
But who am I kidding, we were never together
You were just a hope, a dream, a sunny spot amidst a sea of stormy weather
Please try not to take this wrong
This poem is just my thoughts in song

A jumbled mess if ever there was one
A mess I hope is sorted when I'm done
I know these words sound mean, condemning
But understand that they're just stemming
From that madness that's consumed my soul
A madness that has taken quite a toll
But never take this as goodbye
Wipe the tears, please don't cry
Because whatever happens in the end
Know that I will always be your friend
You're just too important to me
To push away so selfishly
Just because you loved another first
How I wish he had been me
That things had turned out differently
That our situations were reversed
I really want for you to know
That though I'll try my best not to show
The love for you I harbor in my heart
I'll always hope that our romance
Still stands another chance
And in your life I'll play a major part

Forest Fire

Faded wraiths standing tall
Spectres of what once was all
This world ever knew
Ashes black upon the earth
Nature's tears, for what they're worth
Can't forgive the horrors that we do
How can we sit here and pretend
That we could not prevent this end
When we're the ones who caused it all along
A cigarette idly cast
Raging fire, spreading fast
Human habit clearly in the wrong
How quickly we drive by
Barely glancing to the side
Not wanting to admit what we have done
We claim that we all tried our best
And hold the sorrow in our chest
But in our hearts we know that we still run
From the truth of our sins
Unforgivable actions
That one day we will finally answer for
When nature decides to settle the score

Masks

I wipe the dirt from the window
To see a sky that was never blue
I pull the mask from your face
To reveal what I always knew
How does it feel to be naked
Your lies bore for all to see
How does it feel, can you bear it
To be broken as you broke me
But even vengeance tastes bitter
For you never had a heart
And my weakness will always be you
Even after you tore me apart
So like a fool I approach you
Regret swimming in my eyes
And I fall for the same old tricks
As you don the same old disguise
When will I learn my lesson
When will this cycle end
Can't I just win or lose this game
Instead of playing it over again
I guess I'll don my own mask
And watch as you don yours
Because love has never been fair
In anything but war

A Frankenstein Heart

Why is life so complicated
Don't you know how long I've waited
For a little taste of happiness
Now I feel so hurt and jaded
A Frankenstein that you've created
Broken hearted how can I progress
Look at you heartless and cruel
Thread spinning from the spool
Pretending you can piece me back together
You say you feel guilt and regret
But it's too late so just forget
The two of us are done now and forever
When you cheated did you think
That I would never find the link
Between you and your second lover
Did you think I wouldn't know
That the signs wouldn't show
And your infidelity I'd not discover
Now it's your turn to feel the pain
That emptiness you can't explain
Is the love I filled your heart with all these years
How does it feel to be alone
To hold a sin you can't atone
And find your heart filling up with tears
Perhaps you got what you deserve
Still I can't help but preserve
The memories of what I shared with you
And somewhere deep inside
The darkness where your soul resides
I know that secretly you hold them too

Away

You once were the cut but now you're the blade
Slumbering in my wrist
Remember that time we never kissed
Watch the blood well from the skin
Your daily wine
Drink it in
Scars are wounds that never heal
They're memories you can see and feel
There was once a time
Long ago
You feared that I might hurt you
How could you know you'd be the one
To break my heart in two
Halves of a whole
Derelict
They weren't enough to sate
The guilt you felt
You called it hate
So you broke it again
And then
You stomped it to dust
I thought I could trust
Your smile
But all the while
You were twisting the knife in my back
It seems you have a knack
For causing pain
Watch the blood drain
Away

Resolute

Understand that no one cares as much about you
No one will ever love you like I do
And you say that you don't feel the same
But I know how to play this game
And win
There is no end
Only a start
And it begins within my heart
With this aching that I feel
An emptiness your love would fill
Don't go and try to run from me
Because in time you'll only see
That which you flee will soon be found
Because this world we share is round
You can't escape your destiny
You know that you belong with me
Side by side and hand in hand
It's time for you to understand
That no one cares as much about you
No one will ever love you like I do
Deny it all that you want to
But I'll always love you
As you'll come to love me

Shipwreck

See the storm clouds gathering
Banshee wind is whistling
So loud
Black waters reaching for the sky

Too much for a mortal man
Captain of a ship that can
Not live
But for hope he has to try

Land ho! Calling from the nest
A fog bank lingers to the west
At last
A haven to escape to

But closer signals siren's cries
Black teeth from the waters rise
To feed
Upon the bodies of the crew

Life is a shipwreck on the shore
Of a deserted land
You're the sole survivor and
What's more
The ship's hold
Was filled with gold

Countless pebbles on a beach
Tide water's out of reach
For some
While others drown beneath the waves

Seagulls calling overhead
Keening for the dead

That float
While others sink to wat'ry graves

Flotsam floating in the bay
A dark reminder of the day
That you
Became stranded on this strange land

You were just a galley boy
So poor that you could not enjoy
Your life
But now a fortune lies in your hand

Life is a shipwreck on the shore
Of a deserted land
You're the sole survivor and
What's more
The ship's hold
Was filled with gold

Just how cruel is destiny
To leave you with the ship's hold key
While you
Will never get to use it

An irony that drives you mad
An empty land, a fortune had
That's life
You're a toy to amuse it

You understand what you must do
The only option left to you
That's right
Cast the key into the sea foam

Now you're free, unburdened by

The weight of the world and the sky
What's left
A private island to call home

Life is a shipwreck on the shore
Of a deserted land
You're the sole survivor and
What's more
The ship's hold
Was filled with gold

The King of Hearts

Once upon a time, there was a man
He stood on the podium, his heart in his hand
He held it high for all the people to see
He said this is what you get, this is me
It stood there beating in the frosty air
Each thump of emotion to all laid bare
It wormed through their skin and into their souls
Found their own spongy hearts and filled in the holes
And then arose a feeling that none could explain
The felt the man's love and they felt his pain
He said I am your leader and I am your king
But I'm still just a man stumbling
Looking for purpose, justice, and light
Making mistakes and making them right
So sow your fields and drive your flocks
Fell your trees and break your rocks
Try to eek a living from this land
And never be ashamed to hold your heart in your hand
For that is the fate of human kind
Looking for happiness but all they find
War and famine, death and decay
And so they turn to me and say
Ease our hardships, end our suffering
Won't you make things right O' King
So next time happiness is what you demand
Remember this heart that I hold in my hand
Hear it beat and feel it break
And know that my happiness is what you take
For like you I am nothing but a man
Taking what I've got and doing the best that I can

The Merchant's Daughter

Do you hear the waves crashing upon the distant shore
Drowning grains of sand with their liquid roar
They're trying to tell a story, of a time long long ago
And if you listen closely you'll hear their tale of woe
Once there stood upon this beach a lighthouse tall and bright
Steering ships away from doom through the inky night
And at the foot of the lighthouse sat a village in a bay
And there took place a story people speak of to this day

It began with a girl, a daughter, and an heir
Her father a wealthy merchant with more money than love or care
But he always had one vice, that being his daughter's hand
And who he felt was worthy, or not, to fit it with a wedding band
And as it goes with such stories, there was certain man
Who held the daughter's heart, but did not fit the father's plan
He was not but a scoundrel, no money to his name
But that did not diminish his glamour or his fame

For the man, he was a pirate, known throughout the land
Not for rape and pillage, but for helping the common man
With his ship he robbed the wealthy, then spread his loot among the poor
On his head amassed a bounty, and in his heart the girl's amour
By night he'd scale the walled estate and to the daughter's room
Where they'd plan by shadow beneath the stars and moon
And so arose between them a boldly constructed plot
To steal the father's gold and flee together so not to be caught

Alas word of the treachery reached the father's ear
And he devised his own plan to make the pirate disappear
His daughter he locked in her bedroom, a hired gun at the door
And stationed around the estate he placed thirty soldiers more
Then he watched the shadows lengthen waiting for the sun to set
And for his daughter's lover to fall into his net
Finally the subtle sound of footfalls split the night
And the desperate daughter began to sing the sorrow of her plight

"Flee my luckless lover, run far away from me
Do not let your death here be your destiny
Sail to the horizon and fade into the distant sun
For beyond this wall lies only death at the bad end of a gun
You cannot fight this many men, it's hopeless, turn away
Don't try to be hero, it's alright, I'll be okay
Know I'll always love you as I know you love me
But here we have to part, so turn your heart back to the sea"

Unfortunately danger is a pirate's oldest friend
And love can dull the sharpest wits and turn a mind on end
Therefore the daughter's lyric plea fell deaf upon his ears
And her pirate lover cast aside his reservations and his fears
Then when the night grew black enough to hide his form from view
The pirate slipped over the wall and did what he had to do
Silently he kneeled and from his boot a dagger drew
Then one by one, with graceful ease, he thirty gunman slew

Without a second wasted he scaled the manor wall
And to the balcony hoisted himself, heavy heart and all
Without a thought he dispatched the lone guard by the door

And to his arms the daughter leapt, heedless of the blood and gore
A flash and dull roar sounded, then an endless moment spanned
And the father stood in the doorway, a smoking pistol in his hand
The daughter clutched her chest where a ruby river flowed
Then slackened in her lover's grip as her heartbeat quickly slowed

The father stared in horror at the thing that he had done
But his grip never faltered as he held onto his gun
The pirate let his dead love go and his grief echoed through the bay
Then burning eyes locked on the father, vowing to make him pay
Like an angry bull he charged and the father fired his gun
Five times he fired and hit his mark, but couldn't halt the pirate's run
Strong hands wrapped around his neck and squeezed till his eyes turned misty gray
Then the pirate lay down beside his love and his life gently slipped away

The Pirate's Life

We're the scoundrels of the sea
Cutthroats, brigands, or what have ye
Lawless men, doing as we please
Plundering ships upon the high seas
We let the Jolly Roger fly
As from the crow's nest we do spy
A merchant ship horizon bound
Upon which loot is to be found
All extra canvas is hoisted high
Stealing wind from anxious skies
And so the cat and mouse begins
A race for which there's but one end
As we draw nearer, stern to bow
We fire a warning shot aft of their prow
And knowing we've caught them, they drop all speed
And their captain emerges to beg and to plead
He barters for mercy with dignified grace
Belying the fear in the flush of his face
For under his nose twenty cannons lie waiting
Black powder maws with a bloodlust for sating
He knows they won't fire and send his ship under
For no pirate sinks a vessel with plunder
But he and his crew are expendable fodder
To be cut and tossed bleeding into the water
As captain their souls and those of their families
Lie in his hands, and those of their enemies
And so every word uttered is carefully weighed
Lest a slip bring a price that cannot be paid
But we cannot spare the time for his eloquence
Lest a navy ship spy us and dole out the consequence
So we brandish our swords and blunderbuss high
Hooting and howling aloud to the sky
Then we drop boards from our deck to theirs
And dash across hunting like hounds after hares

Blood stains the waters and screams pierce the skies
As we murder and slaughter with gold in our eyes
Then quick as it started the horror is through
And their ship is left empty of cargo and crew
The gangplanks are lifted and the cannons are stowed
And we set sail once more with a much richer load
We are the scoundrels of the sea
Cutthroats and brigands or what have ye
Landlubbers languor while we sail free
That's the pirate's life for me

The Root of Depression

Choose your words more carefully
Lest they hurt someone
You don't understand how easily
Hearts can be undone
One misplaced word is all it takes
To plant the seeds of sorrow
Which, watered by the tears I shed,
A wilting flower follows
Depressing bloom of brittle leaf
Decaying in my breast
A weed not soon uprooted, though many try their best
A predatory pestilence
At worst it kills it's host
Had only you thought before you spoke
You'd not be speaking with my ghost

Golden Sun

Golden sun
Won't you shine
Won't you shine on me
With your light
Drive back the night
And set me free
Through the shadow
Through the shade
Piercing rays
Like a blade
Ripping through the storm clouds above my head
With your light
Reveal the lies
Golden sun
Won't you rise
And pull me from my bed
Let the nightmares fall away
Let daydreams fill the day
Finally life has begun
So set me free
Shine on me
Golden sun

This is War

Flames crackling
Chains shackling
Madmen cackling
Heroes tackling
Problems of a world gone wrong
Swords flashing
And shields bashing
And teeth gnashing
And men clashing
Fighting just to prove they're strong
The Earth's turning
And the world's burning
And the seas are churning
But no one's learning
And the men are dying
Leaving children crying
While the wives are trying
But the bullets keep flying
And there's bodies piling
Corpses smiling
Maggots styling
While peace is whiling away
The land is bleeding
And the crows are feeding
And there's people pleading
With the monsters leading
But no one's heeding what they say
Blood and gore
It's what what's we're fighting for
There's really nothing more
Though we may implore
That it's for land and lore
Perhaps to free the poor
But the truth is war is just a game

We're all guns for hire
Bathed in blood and fire
Idols to admire
And though we conspire
To change what peace requires
We will never tire of the same

Balance

Look inside and you will see
The chains that bind you and the key
Unlock yourself with honesty
To find that truth will set you free
Face the fear and face the pain
Face the guilt and face the shame
Face the grief and face the lies
Illusions left unrecognized
Release ties to reality
And transcend the bounds of your body
Let it go
Let it flow
Out your body and your soul
Feel the streams of energy
Unblock your chakras
Free your chi
Find your center
Look inside
Peace shall enter
And reside
Reflect and break the bonds that bind
To balance spirit, body, and mind

Sink or Swim

You took me to the ocean
And you waited for the tide
Then you tied me to your stony heart
And watched the water rise
Like a fool I sat there trusting you
Thought you'd never let me down
But I misjudged your character
For you let me drown

Sink or swim
It's how you lose or how you win
Love or try
It's how you live and how you die
Life is lived on a boat
With a hull full of holes
When it sinks, it's best you float
Lest you drown in a sea of souls

The water creeps across my chest
And yet I do not flinch
I just watch you sit there watching me
As the water rises inch by inch
Sweet surf strokes the stubble
That grows upon my chin
And I think maybe you'll save me now
But no, not even then

Sink or swim
It's how you lose or how you win
Love or try
It's how you live and how you die
Life is lived on a boat
With a hull full of holes
When it sinks, it's best you float

Lest you drown in a sea of souls

Bilge water bubbles beneath my nose
I take one last salty breath
And through rippling water I see your face
The sweet harbinger of my death
I feel alone and overwhelmed
No purpose and no way
Perhaps it's best the water's here
To wash the pain away

Sink or swim
It's how you lose or how you win
Love or try
It's how you live and how you die
Life is lived on a boat
With a hull full of holes
When it sinks, it's best you float
Lest you drown in a sea of souls

In the deep silence reigns
And darkness is the norm
While high above me sunlight flickers
Bright, alive, and warm
I stretch my arms to their full length
I try to reach the light
But I only seem to sink
Farther out of sight

Sink or swim
It's how you lose or how you win
Love or try
It's how you live and how you die
Life is lived on a boat
With a hull full of holes
When it sinks, it's best you float

Lest you drown in a sea of souls

Pressure building in my lungs
This is where my end begins
And I'm still hoping that you'll come
Even as my vision dims
Dark abyss, my watery grave
How could you let me down
Never more to live or love
You let me down

Sink or swim
It's how you lose or how you win
Love or try
It's how you live and how you die
Life is lived on a boat
With a hull full of holes
When it sinks, it's best you float
Lest you drown in a sea of souls

Jackals

Crossed fingers, twisted tongues
Fire burning in your lungs
Wishing you could shout
Tell everyone how you feel about
Their dirty games
But you feel ashamed
'Cause you know you've taken part
In their shifty ways
And their moral greys
And it's heavy on your heart
Because you understand the anarchy it promotes
We're just jackals tearing at each other's throats
Bloated egos, arrogance
Take what we want with impudence
Stepping on the lesser man
King of the hill, law of the land
We try to change until we see
Another opportunity
To increase money, power, fame
Any cost for any gain
Gold lined pockets filled with coin
From empty stomachs we purloin
We cut the earth to watch it bleed
All for want and naught for need
Back to bestial tendencies
We'll never learn until we see
We're jackals, vultures, vermin, sharks
And primal nature fuels our hearts

Everything

What is this madness that my life's become
How did it twist from the perfection that it started from
It's now a rose without the bloom
A thorny stem that's wrapped around my heart
And it's starting to consume
My very soul; it's tearing me apart
Why can't you drop the fabrication
Why can't you tell me straight
I'm lost in aberration
And I can't translate
The monster that I see
With who you used to be
I'd give you anything
I'd do whatever it takes
But you must be willing
To correct your mistakes
You have to sacrifice
All good things have their price
Am I not worth more
Than the things you dumped me for
Just forget about the rest and think of me
That may sound conceited but it's the only way you'll see
Just look into yourself and find out how you feel
You said you loved me, well here's your test to know if that was real
Let's run away
Let's leave this world behind
Forget today
It's time to find
What tomorrow can bring
Maybe it's everything
And everything I need is you
Can't I be your everything too

Scarred

Headphones in, world out
This time there can be no doubt
Tonight is the night I snap for good
Parents screaming in the other room
Fire burning in me ready to consume
Problem child always misunderstood

Just a matter of time before they come to blows
Hide my sorrow in a hoodie but my anger still shows
I quiver in frustration, know there's nothing I can do
Until my flight turns to fight and I finally turn to
The silk wrapped blade in my underwear drawer
Ball my fist, bare my wrist, and watch the blood poor
Forget anxiety, I finally control the pain I feel
This is a wound unlike my soul I know in time can someday heal

I'm a teenage girl of ill repute
Dad's a drunk and Mom's a prostitute
Seems to be a curse to be alive
Seventeen scars that will never fade
A broken heart and a razor blade
Only time will tell if I survive

The door bursts open and my dad stumbles in
Holding a leather belt and a bottle of gin
I try to hide the blood but he's already seen
And he draws his arm back and I start to scream
He pauses for a moment after several hard blows
And I think the torture's over till he takes off his clothes
My wrist is still bleeding as he has his way
Then the room starts spinning and my skin turns grey

A polished coffin and empty pews
A provocative blouse, a bottle of booze
Did I really think there would be more
A disturbed girl commits suicide
That's the story of how I died
Guess I should have watched what I wished for

Hall of Mirrors

Does he have a face?
Does he have a name?
How dare he place a stake on the heart I claim
Stand behind me
I'll be your shield
I'll be your knight
Let him try to hurt you
Let him try to fight
But how can I guard
Against the unseen attack
How can I fend off
The knife thrust in my back
What did he offer
That I did not already give
You're so ready to love
But so unready to live
Jumping from arm to arm
From heart to heart
What about the family I wanted to start
I guess I'm washed up
I'm old news
He's fresh meat
I'm overused
I guess I was nothing but the next thrill
The next kill
But now I'm dead to you
And he's something new
Except he's not
Because he's been here the whole time
Pretending to fit the friendship paradigm
While always plotting to steal your heart
And you were so willing
It was so thrilling
To watch me fall apart

We all try to play the victim
But we're all guilty here
Pointing fingers
In a hall of mirrors
And we find that the face is our own
The name the same
Betraying ourselves
Life's a twisted game

The Friend Zone

Oldest of old
The story that's told
To children around the fire
A tale of two
Call them me and you
And the journey we transpired
Thick with sorrow
And broken hearts
A tragedy of romance
It all began
When I approached you
With a tentative advance
A first sight love
Was there ever one
Or at least it was for me
Alas for you
The same was not true
Thus the love could never be
But firm in will
And creative in way
I played the love struck fool
I persevered
To pressure the coal
Into a precious jewel
I dogged you by day
And inquired by night
And soon acquired your trust
A friend, no more
Trapped just before
The line crossing into lust
Apologies
From you to me
Saying love lay not in your heart
I was left alone

Unloved and unknown
From the inside torn apart
Forever doomed
To give, not receive
To love you but not you me
A painful place
So close yet so far
To that which will never be
A story of
One sided love
To many it is known
By hated name
As they too became
Victims of the friend-zone

Suicide Note

Sweet landscapes that I used to paint
Now deserts in my head
Endlessly I wander with a world weary tread
Friendships lost and soon forgotten
Too painful to recall
Seems as if finally I've lost it all
I recede within a sullen self
Loneliness the norm
My frigid heart no longer capable of keeping me warm
Bullies bandy insults
Like blades thrust through my heart
Apathy the haven to which I now depart
The sunlight seems to only show
The shadows and the pain
A distant flickering beyond a broken window pane
No loved ones to love me
Just scars that don't fade
Memories mocking mistakes that I've made
No purpose to guide me
No reason to stay
No will and no fight left to face a new day
Don't morn my departure
Those that still care
Don't waste time and breath on blessings and prayer
I did this for you
To spare you the pain
Of talking me through tough times again and again
No more obligation
Goodbye, it's my time
With love, salutations, my death bell has chimed

Cognitive Casualty

Lost and lonely
Seems I'll only
Live a life of one
Sometimes I wonder
If I'm living under the gun
Voices screaming in my head
Can't seem to agree
I try to sort them out
But turns out every voice is me
Squabbling for recognition
Gobbling up suppositions
All looking for a way out of the pain
Sanity spiraling down the drain
Heart shattered and broken
Head battered, broke open
Emotions in turbulent frenzy outspoken
I'm a wreck of uncertainty
Hurt inadvertently
Hoping escape can be won
Ignorance blinding me
Pretense unwinding me
Slowly I'm being undone
Terminus closing in
Death's decomposing grin
Reaping a crop long past dead
Consumed by the war in my head

Cracks

It seems like breaking is all the heart's good for
And I don't think I can take it anymore
But another crack divides my stony heart
Feel the dust as it shrouds my lungs
Too much sorrow for one so young
Now throw the final blow and watch me fall apart

I thought you loved me
I guess I should have seen
The past repeating
And known we never could have been
I was a fool to
Give my heart to you
Without a guarantee I'd get yours too

Life is a labyrinth with monsters at every turn
And our solution is to break the walls and watch it burn
But what's left to live for when we're through
Love is the string that guides us through the maze
Circumventing the rubble and the blaze
I thought that it would lead me straight to you
But how could I have guessed
The apathy that you possessed
As you struck the match and set the string on fire
My heart the dynamite
The fuse you set alight
Blown to pieces by the object of my desire

I thought you loved me
I guess I should have seen
The past repeating
And known we never could have been
I was a fool to
Give my heart to you

Without a guarantee I'd get yours too

It seems like breaking is all the heart's good for
Each crack the ruins of another paramour
Too shattered to bear the weight of the pain
Glass organ, shards tearing through my chest
Blood welling, pouring at your request
Watch it as it swirls down the drain
Empty body, empty soul
Remnant of the man you stole
Waiting for another to steal me back
Then I'll watch you reach for me
Attracted by your jealousy
I'll smile when I see your cold heart crack

I thought you loved me
I guess I should have seen
The past repeating
And known we never could have been
I was a fool to
Give my heart to you
Without a guarantee I'd get yours too

Sacrifice

Lay me down on the operating table
Strap me down tight so I'm not able
To struggle against the knife you place against my chest
Draw some blood as you start to split me open
Steady hands slowly slice through my skin
And find it's worn thin from fending off a world I detest
Muscle rending underneath the scalpel
Fibers flailing like thread cut from the spool
White ribs showing scars from you previous attempts
Find my eyes are empty and unfeeling
As you violate my body by revealing
The secrets of my heart with your experiments
Organs pushed aside reveal its presence
Beating origin you seek to silence
Surgery to save your life by ending mine
Don't balk now, you're standing on the threshold
Dig in deep because you're about to behold
The terminus of all you sought to realign
Don't knock me out with a plethora of potions
Open my heart and drown in my emotions
Brace yourself or the tears will wash you away
Take it now and crush it with a fury
End my pain and finally set yourself free
Don't hesitate, now's not the time to delay
What are you doing, taking off you clothes here
Stop, remove that blade from your breast dear
Horror upon my face as I comprehend
You pull your beating heart from your chest and
Place it right where mine used to rest, then
Sow me up as I watch your life slowly end
I struggle against the bonds that restrict me
But I commanded that you bind them tightly
Now it seems my words become my vice
You heart beats against my ribs at great speed

Lending strength to my limbs and now I'm freed
But I'm too late, you're gone, such sacrifice

Envy

Young couples smiling
As they walk hand in hand
My jealousy growing
They can't understand
Love seems so widespread
Sorrow unknown
While I lie here broken
Unloved and alone
And I love you
Like you'll never know
Even when I tell you
You just tell me no
Rejection a chisel
Shaping my heart
But amateur fingers
Just break me apart
Food left uneaten
Like dust on my tongue
Sleep lost to tears spent
Too frail for one so young
A war zone in my head
When I lay eyes on you
Conflicting emotions
I don't know what to do
Should I feel happy
To find you so near
Or lost in the terror
Of the rejection I fear
Each day a struggle
To mask all the pain
Like the tears that threaten
To pour like the rain
That's when I see them
Carefree and gay

And my envy smolders
Because I can't look away
Young couples smiling
As they walk hand in hand
Ignorant of heartbreak
They can't comprehend

Second Chance

You had your chance and you knew it
I made an advance, but you blew it
My love blazed while his smoldered
But you set us shoulder to shoulder
And you weighed and you measured
To see who played and who pleasured
But couldn't face the results
Face it now, we're adults
You made the easy decision
Took the lesser collision
The one that left fewer ripples in the pond of your life
Kept you balancing on the sharp side of a knife
I told you jump and I'd catch you, but you lacked the gut
Did you really expect that you wouldn't get cut
And now you're falling and bleeding
I hear you bawling and pleading
But I'm a long way down in the dirt where you left me
And my arms are closing around a girl who finally gets me
So you better fall fast if you wish to endeavor
To right the wrongs of the past 'cause I'm not waiting forever
I've got a heart that needs loving
I don't need pushing and shoving
Leave him now, no delaying
Hearts are too fragile for playing
So pull me close and just kiss me
'Cause I know that you've missed me
Show me you care
Second chances are rare

Your Move

You know we're meant to be
You know it's destiny
And if you don't believe in fate then just believe in me
I've got solutions for your issues
I've got tissues for your tears
And I just wish you'd let me lay to rest your worries and your fears
'Cause I can love you like no other could
Love you like a lover should
Love you with a passion that you know no other ever would
Unlike that wholly inconsiderate
Affectionately illiterate
Prick who only seems to care when you're fed up with his constant shit
He's a font of immaturity
A harm to your insecurity
How can he compare to the bond we share every moment you're alone with me
And I get the hesitation
But it fills me with frustration
When he hurts you and you reward him with unyielding infatuation
And I know I'd be the better man
But what you have to understand
Is that you have to make the first move to unite the ground on which we stand

Humpty Dumpty Man

I thought that love was only true in fairy tales
And then I met you
Now I know
Life has a bitter sense of humor
Like Tantalus tortured you were placed within my grasp
Only to be torn away at the apex of my infatuation
Perfection rendered on the tip of an artist's pencil
But no paper within reach
How can it surprise you that I'm driven mad
I've shed more tears than April
But May never blooms
And my heart bears more cracks than parched earth
How can you call me whole
I am broken beyond repair
A Humpty Dumpty man
And you my wall
What hope have I to meet a girl with more means than a king
Horses and men
I am their failure
And yours too
I tried to be your fairy tale
But I'm just a nursery rhyme
If children only knew

Stealing Sleep

Shadows dancing on the wall
Midnight revelers of my imagination
I hardly even notice them
In lieu of my happiness and frustration
For something plagues my mind
Or rather someone fills my thoughts
And sleep has long eluded me
Though I've quaffed many drowsy droughts
How I wish to wrap her in my arms
Instead of just my dreams
I guess that's why I cannot rest
Want plucking at my heart strings
She is a thief of master skill
For every night she steals my sleep
And somehow it doesn't seem justified
To trade her for counting sheep
But sleep is like a time machine
Turning today into tomorrow
So I succumb to the Sandman's beckonings
To bypass my foolish sorrows
And when the sun rises in the morning
And I wake up with a smile
I'll be so much closer to seeing her again
That the sleep will have been worthwhile

Wooden Heart

He tells her he loves and she kisses him
Then he shoves her back and she says she misses him
And I'm ready to retaliate
When he starts to humiliate her
But she leans in through the pain
Past the ridicule and the hurt
And she kisses him again
And my eyes just can't avert
I'm locked in loneliness
And only this madness keeps me going
And the effort I expend to keep the insanity from showing
Has got me all strung out
And I'm just about ready to rant and shout
Because my opportunity is diminishing quick
And I'm starting to feel sick
Getting dizzy, stomach's heavy
And the levees just broke
Tears washing down my face
I'm starting to choke
On the lump in my throat
And your ship can't float when it's full of holes
My wooden heart’s stranded on rocky shoals
And I'm doing my best to patch the perforations
But every time she touches him it sends reverberations
Arcing through my body and the damage gets worse
I can't even escape the pain in the solace of verse
Hail the victor, let him win
I give up and I give in
So strike a match and light the tinder
Hungry flames coughing cinders
My wooden heart the fuel they crave
Let smoke and ashes mark my grave

Move On

Such anger I can't fathom writhing deep within me
Rising to the surface to be unleashed violently
Once upon a friendship turned to hate and homicide
At least that's where my thoughts like to reside
You say I've changed, that I'm a monster, not the man I used to be
You're right, I changed the moment you said that you loved me
My soul's been hurt and twisted beyond recognition
Battered and broken into a most dilapidated condition
If you could even glimpse it through the cracks in my heart
You'd be driven to tears and your sanity too would depart
Can you really blame me for the abhorrence I harbor
When I have to watch him enjoy all that I yearn for
Knowing he doesn't deserve one single moment
Of the love that you give him while I idle in torment
The ghost of a ring on your finger, I ache
Reminding me cruelly just what's at stake
I feel like I'm in check and it's not even my move
You know my love is greater, so what have I left to prove
Change is the nature of life, it's a blessing
So why do you fear the act of progressing
Why do you cling to a horse long past dead
Kicking it, hoping it will raise its head
And maybe it will stand up and gallop again
Face it, that race has reached its end
So move on, I'm waiting and willing to try
You won't regret it and neither will I

Sole Alternative

I think it's time I quit pacing on the sidelines and get my head in the game
Because we both know I still love and I know you feel the same
But you're content to leave me waiting while you wrestle your emotions
And I'm watching seas of fish pass, a lonesome vessel in the ocean
Getting kind of seasick from the back and forth motion
Push me back, then pull me closer, undecided devotion
Fuck mind games, I'm tired of putting my heart on the line
I'm not a fucking option, I think it's finally time
Look through my eyes and the decision is clear
While he's been back and forth, I've always been here
Countless nights he stole your sleep, icy heart burning colder
And I'd comfort you as you'd weep, head resting on my shoulder
He just pulls at your heart strings like a puppet master
Fucking bastard doesn't really care
And I'm not looking to share with a prick who's just looking to stick his dick in your downstairs
A relationship isn't just a race to the sack
It's taking what's given and it's giving back
And I know you say you love him and he says he loves you too
But love isn't said with words, it's expressed in the things you do
What has he done for you
Here's a little clue
Nothing
He's done nothing at all
Think real hard and try to recall
Maybe happiness existed once upon a time
Back when childhood insisted that love was sublime

But when reality conflicted with the carefree paradigm
Did he really hold his hand out and help you climb
Or did he drag you through the dirt chasing foolish dreams
Ignoring when you hurt, pretending not to hear the screams
Did he chain you down with pity, lock your heart up with guilt
If you ask me princess it seems like a pretty shitty castle you've built
I think it's time to pack up and move on
Forget the past because it's gone
And I'm here and I'm now
And I'm waiting best I can
But I just can't allow you to be with that excuse for a man
I need to see you happy again, confident in romance
And I think I can get you there if you'll just give me the chance

Consolation Prize

I want to catch all of your tears
But there are too many
And anything I do seems too little
It'll pass in time
I'm sure
But not really
Sometimes there is no cure
Call it silly
But the only hope
It is to cope
And don't give in
Or you won't begin to heal
It's good to feel
You should until it's too much
Such pain that you can't win
Even if you fight
That's where I come in
So you might stand a chance
To advance in life
Progress through strife
I confess I like
To imagine an us
Thus I try
But I'm not a guy
Who will fiddle with a broken heart
Fragile things tend to fall apart
So I'll bide my time
Sit and ride the line
And when you feel you can
Reach out and love again
I'll be here for you
To love you too

Stranger Relationships

I once looked out my window
And saw you in the shadows
Watching and thinking that you were not seen
And I began to ponder
I sat back and I wondered
How you had lapsed into this sick routine
You could walk up to her
Man up and talk to her
Instead you stalk her
That beauty queen
She's just a person
And there are people worse than you
She would be lucky to
Find someone more obsessed
I see you peeping
And just for safekeeping you
Take pictures of the view
As she gets undressed
She must be so naive
To leave her window wide
Unless there's nothing to hide
Because she sees you too
She likes to be admired
She's tired of being ignored
And she feels so adored
When she strips for you
A peeping Tom
And an attention whore
There must be something wrong
With this twisted world
Such strange relationships
That somehow exist
While I remain alone
I'll never understand this place I call my home

Red Riding Hood and the Wolf

Ignorant in innocence roaming remiss beneath the trees
A basket of baked goods consistently clacking against her knees
Fledgling figure bundled beneath a cloak of vibrant red
Oblivious of the peril posed by the simply spotted thread

Saber sharp teeth craving meat fresh from the living
A predator preying voracious violence unforgiving
Saliva slathered tongue licking lips in anticipation
Ember eyes glowing, bloody bulbs of expectation

Preparing to pounce and freely feast seeing none around
The hunger worn Wolf falters as his ears espy a sound
The regular report of steel striking wood
Means a lumberjack lingers near the girl with the hood

Not to be beaten and let lunch get away
The witty Wolf sees the child's course does not stray
So rather than risk striking and suffering retaliation
He hurries along to see what waits at her destination

Withered and wrinkled, a time tested figure
She shuffles around, world weary, without vigor
A hermetic home built far beyond observation
A simply seized meal made without tempting vindication

Silent and swift, dangerous and deadly, he strikes
Ripping and rending, feral fangs sharper than pikes
Grandmother gobbled quickly and quietly up
A tonic of tea still steaming in her cup

Flesh flavored breath and jagged jaws gaping
Fatigue filled yawn from his bulging belly escaping
The Grandmother's bed beckons with soft silk and lace
So the Wolf slumbers beneath blankets that cover his face

Heedless of the harm sleeping softly inside
Red Riding Hood pushes the old door open wide
Stepping softly she works her way straight to the bed
Where the Wolf dozes deep under silken thread

Hearing husky snores slipping out from under the cover
She fears sickness has progressed past the point of recover
So clutching cloth in fragile fingers she gives a tug
And the sheet sinks below the Wolf's whiskery mug

First she sights his enormous ears twitching
Then his ember eyes she spies, open and bewitching
Finally terrible teeth still bearing blood are revealed
And she fears the fact that her Grandma might have been killed

A bloodcurdling breath spent in scream she releases
As the wicked wolf pounces prepared to tear her to pieces
Far off in the forest her howls of horror are heard
By a Woodsman with a heart who is by fear undeterred

Lofty legs striding with speed to her aid
Axe at the ready to taste blood on its blade
He arrives at the cottage with seconds to spare
Red Riding Hood cornered and crying in despair

Muscled tendons tensing, longing to lunge and devour
Forelegs flexing with restrained ripping power
His paws hardly have time to lift from the floor
Before an axe blade bites down and the Wolf is no more

Compassion consoling and gratitude given in turn
Red Riding Hood and the Woodsman hand in hand return
To the vestigial village with words of warning for all
The Tale of Red Riding Hood and the Wolf it was forevermore
called

Pale in Comparison

The sun shines pale when she is near
She makes a day pass like a year
The flowers wilt as she walks by
She leaves a wake of empty eyes
She makes a flute sound like a crow
She makes the rivers cease to flow
With her approach the world falls into penury
A paradox of what it used to be
Silk like sand; mountains low
Sugar bland; and burning snow
Without her here my life is hell
Because compared to her the world is pale

Monster in the Mirror

Feel that chill run down your spine
Hairs on end upon your neck
That feeling that you're being watched
Yet sight no one each time you check
The goose bumps growing on your flesh
That knot inside your gut
The shortness in your quickened breaths
And speed within your lengthened strut
Hear that pounding in your ears
Feel the beating of your heart
Fear is coursing through your veins
Logic and reason torn apart
Foreshadowed in the shadows passed
Whispered in the sounds you hear
Present on your crawling skin
Imminent menace looming near
Monsters of your active mind
Ghosts and goblins, wraiths and fiends
Spectres of your most morbid thoughts
Phantoms of your darkest dreams
They're all converging in your head
A piercing scream cuts through
A suddenly you're all alone
Because the monster you see is you

Couldn't Help Myself

I kicked down the gate and tore down the walls
And in the courtyard of your heart I saw it all
All the love I'd given you
Somehow had made it through
Like a Trojan horse inserted
But forgotten and deserted
My army of emotions still in place
Awaiting orders to attack
Make your heart mine, to take it back
Return it to the rightful hands
To my embrace

You built a fortress
And you set him on the throne
He settled in and he made your heart his home
But like a parasite he sucked it dry
And I stood by
Helpless to help you help yourself
Because I couldn't help myself

I was a warrior who fought against the tide
Of darkness streaming from inside
Your heart, the place where he resides
The place where love and hate collides
I want to free you from the tyranny
I want to set you free
Free to feel and free to love
To govern yourself as you see fit
And he's not it
Dark lord's armies streaming at me
Lonesome soldier, I'm combating
Force of evil, foul hands wrapped around your soul
Trading blows with fiends, black fire
Years pass by and I grow tired
Of this struggle for your heart, to gain control

You built a fortress
And you set him on the throne
He settled in and he made your heart his home
But like a parasite he sucked it dry
And I stood by
Helpless to help you help yourself
Because I couldn't help myself

Now I grow old and he is gone
But I fight on
Only to find the battle lost
He may have left, but he took you
Took your happiness too
I have your heart, but at what cost
Like a castle long abandoned
Dilapidated, but still standing
It's not much, but I can make it something more
'Cause I remember long ago
A girl that I used to know
And her heart, this castle I fought so hard for

You built a fortress
And you set him on the throne
He settled in and he made your heart his home
But like a parasite he sucked it dry
And I stood by
Helpless to help you help yourself
Because I couldn't help myself
I couldn't help myself till I helped you
Time's short but now I'm able
To salvage something stable
From these ruins that he left when he left you
Now you can help yourself
No longer helpless in his hands
You're free to stand
Because I couldn't help myself

Infinite Inches

You say you want to just be friends
But you hold me like a lover
Shoulders, hips, and hands and foreheads
Pressed against each other
And yet when I lean in an inch
To close the gap between our lips
You turn your cheek and laugh it off
As if I didn't try to break the script
And when you leave all rosy glowing
You ask me why I never smile
And I can only shake my head
And fake one through my rising bile
Sometimes I want to push you down
And pin your arms back with my own
And kiss you there with all the passion
Of being alone
But I never give in to the urge
As strongly as it beckons me
Because I want you to want it too
I want for you to need
Not just friendship
Close yet distant
Not just hugs and almost more
I want for you to want to be my girl

The Proposal

Oh lovely Amber so pretty and sweet
With white diamond flashing I kneel at your feet
Three years have I loved you so passionately
And now here before you am I on one knee
With trembling lips the question I pose
"Will you marry me Amber, my redheaded rose?"

Oh charming Edgar so handsome and quaint
With your gold band a gleaming, I quite nearly faint
Three years have I loved you and thought you the one
And now standing before you my heart starts to run
I utter the phrase with a tear in my eye
"Yes Edgar, I will, till the day that I die!"

Forever

There is this story
I know it well
Sometimes I find it too painful to tell
Because it has no end
That is
At least until I die
It started long ago
With innocence and happiness
As stories often do
When a boy and a girl fell deeply in love
Let's call them me and you
I can't pretend to understand
Or know the things you thought
But your feelings were clear nonetheless
You loved me quite a lot
Memories were made and shared
In the time we spent together
I thought it would be forever
Alas the world is cruel
And you as well
Somehow you fell for me
And I for you
But while I continued to love
You found someone new
Except he wasn't
Because you knew him well
A lover you loved before you fell
For me
One night of liquors and nostalgia shared
One mistake that can't be repaired
A mistake I didn't see
For months you played fidelity
Like the innocent girl I knew
If only that were true

Eventually we grew apart
That is you grew away from me
While I refused to let you go
Because we were meant to be
And all that time we spent apart
You never let me know
The sin you committed all those months ago
But truth has a way of getting out
Guilt loosened your tongue and my devout image of you
Was forever crushed
But not my love
Even through sorrow and despair
While I pretended not to care
I did
I hid my feelings from the world
I knew they shouldn't be
Not after what you'd done to me
Hearts can't be changed with will though
So I couldn't let you go
Not where it mattered most
Deep down where my feelings can never hide
The place my tears reside
It's like an ocean now
How did I get here
In a future without you
Why did only my love last
When you said that yours would too
I guess the story's caught up now
No us
No more together
What happened to forever
I'm right here

Greed and Lust and Gluttony

One day I was walking on a cold December day
And I happened on a beggar with an empty belly and empty plate
And before I could approach him with money in my palm
A man in black and suede shoes handed him a pamphlet filled with alms
And with a "bless you" he departed, silver crux hanging from his neck
While the beggar looked defeated and I was left perplexed
So I walked up to the beggar, gave him my money and he looked pleased
And I asked if I could have a look at the tract he'd just received
And when I read the title my heart filled with disgust
For it read "The wealth you seek is found not in coin, but in your heart if the Lord you trust"
I gripped it in such fury, it crumpled in my fist
Prepared to confront the arrogance of the black clad fundamentalist
But after two steps I was halted as a bitter breeze blew by
And I shivered in the frigid air, a cruel reminder of the homeless guy
Pity replaced anger and I removed my coat
Then placed it on his frail shoulders hoping it might help him cope
Then I walked away with a heavy heart feet dragging as if through morass
Just in time to see the theist disappear through an archway of stained glass
Curious, I followed him, though hallowed halls are not my home
A whispered prayer escaped my lips for kindness dictates: when in Rome
And what I saw in that sepulcher of worship to a deity of lies

Sent profanity spewing from my lips and fire from my eyes
For on a little marble pedestal there sat a gilded dish
And as the man in black walked past several coins were relinquished
I'd never felt such loathing or seen such monstrosity
As I stormed back out into the cold away from the hypocrisy
I walked back to the beggar and emptied my wallet into his plate
Then took the crumpled pamphlet and threw it down a damp storm grate
Then I walked home and I laid down within my comfy bed
Feeling like I still owned too much as the beggar starved in my head
The world which we live in is cruel and it's unfair
But we're the ones who make it so because we refuse to share
Through greed and lust and gluttony we make the world poor
Why when we have all that we need must we demand for more
You've only got one life and it's limited in time
So spend it not amassing wealth while others sit and decline
Be content with what you've got and give back what you can
Because wealth is found not in a God, but in the hearts of man

Happily Ever After

I can't describe the way you make me feel
Yet I'll sit here and try to scribe it still
They always call it butterflies
Like vertigo has taken nest
But I decry it's weightier
Like something's finally filled my chest
That cavity, that gaping hole
That emptiness within my soul
That missing link
That missing chink
Within my stony heart
You filled it up, you filled it in
You made it whole once again
A sturdy bond
Never beyond
My reach, even if we part
Most say it fades as time progresses
Fraught with doubts and second guesses
As the novelty of passion melts away
But as my time with you grows longer
I only feel the love grow stronger
Passion burning brighter every day
You are my rock, my firm foundation
Call it cliché with indignation
But when the storm comes rolling in
And turmoil breaks the lonely men
I'll crumble not, but stand my ground
However hard the wind may pound
So long as you remain with me
Forever after happily

Man's Trophy Room

Once I dreamed that I could fly
High up in the clear blue sky
At first I thought it peaceful there
Swaddled in the empty air
Nothing but nature all around
At least till I looked down
That's when my heart sorrow did plague
Soon usurped by boiling rage
As from my lofty perch I spied
A blight upon the countryside
The work of men, the shame of man
The desecration of the land
I saw forests cut and burning
Luscious fields to deserts turning
Gashes gaping in the mountains
Wounds that bleed fuel like steam-punk fountains
Cities of steel like broken bones
Jutting from Earth's broken stones
Asphalt streaming from their bowels
Like poisoned veins black and foul
Snaking out across the land
Foreboding fingers of man's hand
How far his reach extends
How dark a future it portends
I can look no more
And so I choose to soar
Out upon the open sea
A place where man should not be
To the Ocean's farthest reaches
Far from man's polluted beaches
Beyond the belching smoke of progress
Where nature should lie untouched and flawless
Alas to my anger and dismay
Untouched is not man's way

There in the roiling, salty spray
A bulbous mass heaves and sways
A massive mess of amorphous monstrosity
Polymers and monomers cast out in pomposity
An island afloat in unnatural condition
Arrayed in large archipelagic partitions
Dead sea life washed up on its bloated shores
Bodies that number in hundreds of scores
Disgusted I turn to the open sky
Where higher and higher and higher I fly
Through the clouds and the fog
Through the smoke and the smog
Through the troposphere that weather calls home
Through the stratosphere and its tattered ozone
Where space and sky begin to collide
And even here nature can't hide
A sprawling mess of innovation
The product of collaboration
A station incongruous to this realm
And only man could stand at its helm
I try to flee the grotesque contraption
Only to find it a minor fraction
Of the garbage dump that man has made the sky
I weep as space junk leisurely drifts by
And so I leave the Earth behind
To deeper space where I might find
The solitude I seek untouched by man
I fly until I no longer can
A sliver landscape stretches vast
Pockmarked with craters of meteors past
Silent and serene, I bask in its quiet
Free from man's tampering; I dare them to try it
And that's when I see it, cruel silver and gold
Twinkling upon the horizon so bold
One small step backward in learning to live
To coexist with the splendor that nature gives

But man only conquers and man only claims
Ripping and rending he kills and he maims
He does not adapt to his world to survive
He changes his world so that he might thrive
And when he finds nothing alive but himself
He kills that too, one last trophy on his shelf

Warrior Poet

They say to pick your battles
But I'm battling for you
So I don't think it really matters if I win or if I lose
Because I've already hit the bottom
Found it empty, uninviting
I'm alone, your my home, seems like a reason to keep fighting
And it seems these words I'm spilling
Aren't conveying what I'm feeling
But I'm saying what is real and
I am praying that you're willing
To give me one more chance to make it right
Because I know I've made mistakes
But I'll do anything it takes
Adversity a hero makes
Oh tragedy, your heart's at stake
So I won't give up without a fight
Lonesome soldier, getting older
Chance to hold her makes him bolder
But cold shoulder makes him smolder
Anger growing, wrath unchecked
Building tension, condescension
No retention or redemption
His intentions lack attention
Sorrow showing, he's a wreck
I'm that soldier, I'm that fighter
I'm that warrior, that writer
Hoping ink will let me bleed into your heart
So take these words and take this letter
Let it mend things, make them better
And never let us ever drift apart

Darkness

Creeping dusk
Time when the sky is shedding off the husk of day
Half-light fading into cooler shades of grey
The world's almost dark now
The lunar disk is rising
Silver beacon compromising
Nocturnal shadows
Time feels like it slows
And the world's dark now
Starlight flickers, twinkling light
Stark contrast with the inky night
Bright overseers that oversee the activity of humanity
And they just might
Find the world dark now
And maybe darkness has an atmosphere
Of lurking danger we should fear
To run, to hide
To seek the light
But it's alright
To find the world dark now
Yeah it's alright and it's okay
To bid farewell to the light of day
Because
There are diamonds in the darkest deeps
The sweetest dreams in the mind that sleeps
Yeah monsters may call shadows home
But monster's just a term for the unknown
Man's the monster we should fear
And he's not here
Because he prefers the light
So it's alright
The world's dark now

Fight

When circumstance
Says you don't stand a chance
Will you make an advance
And strike a fighting stance
Or will you lie down and die
Refuse to try
Retreat or decry
I will fight
Will you fight
I will fight

I'll set fire to the night
Let the flames burn bright
Then I'll step into the light
Stand up for what's right
I will fight

When oppression tries to silence me
I'll stand against the tyranny
That's the price of being free
Anyone can see
Someone has to make a stand
Bear the blood upon their hand
You must sacrifice for all and
You must fight
Will you fight
I will fight

I'll set fire to the night
Let the flames burn bright
Then I'll step into the light
Stand up for what's right
I will fight

When you stand face to face with the enemy
Vengeance burning, dark energy
He sits helpless on his knees
Begging you for mercy
Will you strike the final blow
Embrace the hate and let it grow
Become the monster or let him go
Don't fight
Will you fight
I will not fight

I'll let the embers dim
Let the shadows have their way
Because the sun will rise again
And welcome a new day
I will not fight

Carry On

He stands above the empty crib that will never be filled again
In his head he hears the cries he'll never hear and then
He cries
Wracking sobs that shake his bones and stir the shards of his shattered heart
A tinkling sound too joyous for the pain that it imparts
Inside
Soft silk blanket, baby blue, runs like water through his hand
But through his soul like sand
And he can't understand why this is happening to him
He thinks he must have made mistakes, earned retribution through them
So he begs a God he's never known and never had faith for
To take his own life in his child's stead, to even the score
And the silence pounding in his ears is too much to bear
An echoing rejection spiraling into despair
He hits the bottle
Hits the throttle
Bad decisions uniting
Slick rain sliding
Car colliding
Father and son reuniting
And the mother is left all alone with her sorrow
Stuck in the past, can't imagine tomorrow
If he'd taken the time to think outside of self-pity
His selfish actions just might have been avoided and then she
Wouldn't have taken her life at the apex of hitting the bottom
Winter, spring, summer, and autumn
Time carries on even if we cannot
So carry on
Don't give in
Don't give up
Say you fought
And just maybe you'll find that though this battle was lost
The war can still be won, no matter how high the cost

Outlet

Whispered words drip from my pencil tip
Shattered lead and eraser shavings mark my slips
Tear stains mar the crisp white page
Swollen white bleeding grey
A sorrowful depiction of my heart
A good place to start
Shifting lines crisscross each other
Merging into one another
Subtle curves that dip and sway
Bold lines that cut straight through the fray
Shifting shadows fill the gaps
I hardly notice time elapse
As I pour my broken soul onto the page
All the sorrow, all the rage
The guilt, the hurt, the tears, the pain
The memories that drive me insane
White knuckled fury keeps me gushing
Emotion from my pencil rushing
Art the outlet for my fractured mind
A template where my demons can be confined
Finally my tears are spent
And locked in lead lies my torment
A physical reflection of my flaws
I tear it into pieces without pause
All my mistakes
Fall like snowflakes
In front of me
And I feel free

A Little Lump of Hope

Somehow hope survives within my head
It doesn't thrive, it's almost dead
But it's still there
A sultry gleam amidst bleak black
Where I can dream of what I lack
If I still dare
Wishes whispered in my mind
Elusive elation I can't seem to find
A flitting face obscured from view
I wish I only knew just who she is
Or if she lives beyond my battered mind
For when I look, a desperate quest
Fraught with heartache and unrest
Loneliness is all I seem to find
Countless times I think her found
My perfect match, together bound
But all she sees of me is what I'm not
A battle lost before it's fought
Weary seems to be the norm
Or at least the calm before the storm
That moment I can't stand it anymore
It starts to rain, it starts to pour
Lightning flashes, thunder booms
I cry, I scream, and violence looms
And then I fall apart
A useless mess of loneliness
Whimpering in hopelessness
A spasm of the heart
But it's still there
Hidden somewhere
A sultry gleam that helps me cope
A little lump of hope

The Heavens

Soft hued darkness of the night
Speckled by spatters of pale starlight
Canvas of the Universe
Too vast to be traversed
By even Man's imagination

A million, billion, trillion leagues
Endless expanses of mysteries
Empty to glances idly cast
A treasure trove of wonders massed
Upon closer examination

Conglomerate clusters of celestial gas
Swirling spheres of unmentionable mass
Invisible entities of inestimable power
But beautiful beyond the most brilliant flower
And all in a pinprick of sky

Galaxies spinning, and churning, and swirling
Planets revolving, evolving, and whirling
Meteors massing, and passing, and crashing
And people excitedly pointing and asking
How fast and how far can we fly

Inky blackness of the night
Pricked by countless points of light
Infinitely picturesque
Even for the most grotesque
Interferences of man

For in every twinkling spot of light
There lies a world untouched by plight
Beyond the petty spats of men
That will endure our rein and then
Ignore our flitting span

Playing God

Hate isn't healing
Too often it's killing
And feelings aren't spared in the process of stealing a life
Stealing a father, a mother, a sister, a brother, a daughter, a son, a husband, or wife
Or maybe just stealing a friend
In the end what you take is a person connected
By strands of affection protected by nothing
But pure unconditional love
And when hearts are infected
And words are inflected
With currents of loathing
Indirectly imposing
The booming voice of some being above
It's these people you hurt
Not just the ones in the dirt
Who feel the effect
Of your hate indirectly
Connecting when push comes to shove
You call me a monster
A monster that loves?
Seems kind of silly to me
Practice your preaching
Or risk only reaching
An audience too blind to see
Tolerance doesn't imply your support
It only requires you do not cavort
As the only opinion worth holding
And when your values conflict
With more sensible edict
Forego the sociopolitical molding
You see people are people
And no sultry steeple
Should try to impose on us all
Because every dictator
And God imitator
Deserves his inevitable fall

Letter to the Pope

Let me start this letter
By explaining that I've never
Put much faith in any god of whose existence I'm assured
Without seeing just an inkling
Of evidence suggesting
That anything he claims to be
Is something more than myths or pretty words
And I'm sure you'll try to tell me
I'm on the highway straight to hell
But see I've never cared for hard rock music either
I just can't seem to get
These planes of judgment you insist
Exist beyond the realm of reason as it be, Sir
And it seems the things you're preaching
Always clash with what school's teaching
Hell they conflict with every action you commit
The hypocrisy you propagate
With every tainted speech you state
Only lowers my opinion of your pulpit
Speaking of that throne
Draped in silk and gilded bones
The ones of enemies you crushed for being sane
How can you sit there in your arrogance
Proliferating intolerance
And claim your hands are clean of everything
And yet your tawdry tome of fairytales
With words from fractured men
Says no man lives and dies
As well as keeping free of sin
So let me make this crystal clear
And get it through that ornate hat your sport
If you look into the neutral mirror
Perfection finds you fall as short
As any mortal man
And that's all you can ever hope to be

Dreams

I remember windswept acres at the mountain's toes
I recall the vibrant grass alive with morning dew
And water ripples spreading under wilting willow boughs
But most of all what I recall is you

You stood amongst the falling leaves
With daisies in your hair
Golden locks like gilded silk
Eyes like ripened pears

I reclined amongst the gnarled roots
On dappled blades of grass
Cool air blowing off the lake
A pool of unbroken glass

I felt intrusive lying there
In my torn and faded jeans
Grass stains in the fabric
And tearing at the seams

You were a vision of perfection
Draped in windswept cotton
Thread the color of my blush
No single stitch forgotten

You did not smile and nor did I
Shadowed gazes steady
Lost within each other's eyes
Whirling pools of heartfelt eddies

My hand outstretched just shy of yours
A microscopic separation
Yet somehow just too great to breach
No matter my desperation

And it was then, as it always is
That I awoke alone
Hand outstretched in empty air
Your name still yet unknown

I almost cry in hopelessness
As I've been known to do
Instead I sigh and close my eyes
So I might dream again of you

My Sun

Back in the days before the sun
Eyes clenched too tight to see its light
Trying to stem the flow of tears
You could say I was depressed

Those were the days of nimbus thoughts
Loneliness sequestered in my heart
Where hope was a thing too surreal to exist
Thus darkness was the future to which I progressed

But like a golden beam of ethereal joy
You pierced the storm clouds of my mind
And bathed the cold desert of my heart
In comforting halos of gilded love

You did not shirk when I lashed out
As I shrunk into the shadows I'd always known
And tried to cast your affections off
Fearing this newfound thing above

You wrapped me tight in consoling arms
Whispers drifting from your lips
Breathing warmth into my soul
To kindle life where there was none

Now the fruitful harvest of my heart
For you to freely feast upon
Sways like wheat within my breast
Beneath your lovely smile, my sun

Confession

Forgive me my transgressions
In faith I'm found chagrined
I come here in confession
For Father, I have sinned

Last night my father raped me
And blasphemy drew forth
From my lips the Lord's name flew
In vain I cursed without remorse

In anger at such treatment
I slew my father first
And shamed by my adultery
Into which I was forcefully coerced

I murdered next my husband
Though loving he had been
For I could not face his judgment
Had he discovered my sin

Then, sorrowed by my actions
I drowned my tears in wine
Gluttonously sating
A thirsty heart and mind

But when I awoke this morning
Stained with blood and self-disgrace
I knew I had to seek you out
And find mercy in your humble grace

By the Father, the Son, and the Holy Ghost
Wipe clean my slate, wash off my sin
I have confessed and now I'm free
An innocent soul again, Amen

Paranoia

I look around at the company
Gathered to dine with me
Companions of many years
And suspicion is creeping
Their treason is reeking
As whispers reach my ears
This is starting to feel like my last supper
They tucker in
My cannibal friends
Flesh and blood
Their feast begins
And they've all got a dagger
Stuck in my back
Pincushion betrayal
Trimming the fat
From my bones
A French revolution
Camaraderie conclusion
With guillotine slashes
I ordain executions
And finally I am alone
In the safety of solitude
Worries fade and I'm soon imbued
With tranquility and sound mind
But in silence a danger waits
Licking its lips
It anticipates
The moment I let down my guard
Paranoia protect me
From those who expect me
To gullibly trust their pretenses of aid
I see the blade that they wield
Sharp tongues that have killed
The faulty fool who lets friends in his heart

Breaking and Entering

She chokes on the scent of formaldehyde thick in the air
Her fractured mind swimming in chemicals
Barely aware
Hardly a care
Apathy clear in her ghostly blank stare
She tries to preserve a past that's already dead
Embalming a memory of childhood deep in her head
But she can't erase
The blood on the sheets
The nightmares that plague her when she falls asleep
No lock on the door
Can make her feel safe
Or shut out the pain at the thought of his face
It's too late to save her
She has already died
She can't shake the thought that he broke her inside
And not just symbolically speaking at that
He physically broke her, no longer intact
That barrier breached and her innocence shattered
Mind overwhelmed and body left battered
Breaking and entering twice by her count
Though the court hardly sentenced a proper amount
To account for the fear that's consumed her whole being
Seeing his face in every shadow and feeling
That healing will take more than time
If indeed she can heal at all from this crime

Seeking Asylum

Once upon a time long past
When youthful vigor still filled my bones
And the world had yet to beat me down
Though it cast words and sticks and stones
I thrived within an ignorance
Convinced that life was rife with joy
And I myself a wizened man
Though life would prove me yet a boy
It was in this time of carefree bliss
That I locked eyes with my better half
The first and last that I would kiss
Sharing life and love and laughs
I took her heart in place of mine
And kept it safe within my breast
I tried to shield it from all pain
Or at least I tried my very best
Alas the world had proved me wrong
Life was not the joy I'd thought
And while her heart was safe with me
My own would come to rot
It happened when she left for work
A day like any other yet
But this one ended with her life
Upon the road a drunk ill-met
I remember well the aftermath
The news received in silent shock
The denial and acceptance too
As I found my ivory tower rocked
My haven buried six feet down
A sanctuary in fresh turned earth
Broken loam my therapist
I poured my soul into that dirt
I go there still though less these days
As aching bones now mirror my heart

Waiting now for the coming end
So different from my sunny start
Seeking asylum through my death
Peace in rest that life denies
Pine box refuge for my bones
But for my soul, I have her eyes
They'll dig my plot there next to hers
Side by side just as in life
Eternity together then
Loving husband and loving wife

The Prostitute

He's whispering in her ear
But she can't hear
Because she taught herself to tune out the world in these moments
The components of her happiness locked away in her mind
Hidden so well she can hardly even find them
After the fact
After the act
The act of bartering her body
And another piece of her soul
She's losing herself
And it's taking its toll
She can hardly even recognize herself in the mirror
But she perseveres
Through the pain and through the shame
Another place another name
Trading sheets and trading faces
But it always feels the same
She used to hate herself but she's grown apathetic
No need to spare emotion for one so pathetic as her
Just like the men that use her for pleasure
They fuck without feeling because she isn't worth that
And they paid her to give pleasure without having to give it back
Little do they know they're only bumping a corpse
Nocrophiliacs screwing without remorse
Because she died long ago when she first sold herself to a stranger
Aware of the shame but not of the danger
But even if she'd known she'd have done it again
Because she needed the money provided by the sin
Money to send to a daughter in need
A daughter abandoned in a time of greed
Now she's struggling to make amends

Throwing her desires to the wind
Relinquishing happiness and forfeiting modesty
Honestly attempting a selfless act
But incapable of keeping herself intact
Because he's whispering in her ear that it'll be okay
That she doesn't have to live like this another day
That he'll care for her financially whatever it takes
But it's too late because she's already slipped away

Philophobia

When I was just five I remember my mother
Weeping her heart into her covers
And clutching a ring to her chest
Faintly I heard
Her whispering words to herself
Asking what she did wrong
When she tried her best
And when I was ten I remember my father
At the kitchen table drowning the last of a bottle of gin
It was all he could do not to cry
And that was when I
Promised that I'd never love
Cause it doesn't exist
Now it's years later and I can't resist
The tempting allure that my body insists that I need
And that I reject
So I compromised with myself
I gave in to lust
But never to trust
That's how I protect
My heart
It's beating in circles
It hurts to be alone
But I can't begin to give in to
Feelings of affection
The feelers of infection
They take root and grow into
Something that I know will just
Hurt me and desert me one day
And then I met you and it all fell apart
You were meant to be a one night stand
Not a function of my heart
But when I woke up and rolled over to see
Not an empty bed

But you staring back at me
I found myself staring back
And caring that you were still there
And then you pushed my hair
Back from my face
And kissed me and I crumbled
Then tumbled from grace
And all those years spent in fear
Suddenly felt like a waste
And I can see the ring pressed to my mother’s chest
My father drowning sorrow as best he knew how
And now I can understand it's not that the love wasn't there
It's because it existed that they even
Cared enough to wallow in
The sorrow that I saw them in
And all those years I followed them
Trying to avoid what I've found
I’ve overcome that fear now

Four Letter Word

Loneliness is all I ever knew until I met you
Tears the only friends I held at night
But something in your smile bespoke of more than simple virtue
And I found myself attracted to your light
A moth transfixed by flame I flew towards danger unperturbed
Because smitten is a four letter word

Oldest of adages to the fool a wise man speaks
A man is nothing more than the company he keeps
So call me blind and call me foolish for heeding siren's calls
But I'm really just a lonely fish in a sea of endless squalls
And I'm searching for a ship that will pluck me from the surf
Because desperate is a four letter word

Virtue is the attribute I'd like to call your best
But you're defined by heartlessness instead
Content to take your pleasure and the organ from my chest
To leave me in the lurch as good as dead
They say it's better to have loved and lost, but I say that's absurd
Because heartbreak is a four letter word

Evolution is a manner in which broken things are righted
But it seems that I've declined instead and thus I feel that I've been slighted
Because lessons learned may come in time and people grow as a result
But I feel I've only lost myself in becoming an adult
Black and white merge into gray while good and bad is blurred
Because love is a four letter word

Keeping the Faith

I find it hard to keep the faith
To force this smile on my face
In the face of all the faithlessness I've faced
When every stranger that I meet
Says "You'll find love, but not in me"
Then ditches me within this rut I've paced a thousand times
They always say she's out there
If I only bide my time
But I find that comfort growing thin
With every year that passes by
My bed feels ever larger
As its emptiness expands
And my nights seem ever longer
As I choke upon the Sandman's sand
I've always walked a lonely road
Hating every step
My heart too deep to call it home
That fate I can't accept
And so at every crossroad
I greet every scarecrow that I meet
Prepared to walk whichever way I'm taken
When I click my feet
Yeah I find it hard to keep the faith
And yet I still do
For what's a thousand failures
If a single victory is you

Exodus of Despair

I fall to the ground, cold earth at my back
Blood wells from a wasteland riddled with flak
It trickles through trenches to pool at my boots
And when I look at my hands, it's on them too
I shudder and find myself choking back sobs
At the thought of the men that I've killed "just doing my job"
I pull a picture from my pocket, yellowed with age
Crease lined from folding and the edges frayed
It settles me down just to feel it in my hand
Taking me back to a time before the killing began
It was a day in the summer, bright sun in the sky
Clouds puffy as cotton balls whiter than white
We stood in the grass and complained of sore feet
As we posed for the picture, me and my family
My mother in the back where her eyes could see all
My father beside her, as broad as he was tall
My sister beside me, eyes full of mischief
Her hands dark with dirt where she'd been digging for worms in the ditches
My brother in front, no smile on his face
Too old for pictures at four years of age
And I in the middle, my smile so cheerful
So ignorant it was, it should have been fearful
Had I only known, the horrors before me
The things that I'd do, the things that I'd see
And suddenly I'm back in the trenches and blood
No blue skies or green grass, just black clouds and black mud
I think back to my lessons from simpler times
Of a black and white world taught from black and white lines
And the sadness wells up as I dwell on my sins
Wondering if I'll ever see my family again
And if I do, will they even connect
The monster they see with the man who left
They'll find no more smiles, just grim faced dejection

I almost give up at that simple introspection
But just before I succumb to self-loathing and despair
Epiphany strikes me right then and right there
That the lessons weren't so simple as first I had thought
It wasn't black and white after all that they taught
But how love can exist amidst so much hate
If someone's willing to fall so another is saved
Where good triumphs evil despite being grey
And every saint is a sinner at the end of the day
I fold up the picture and smile as I stand
Old words in my head, a gun in my hand
They thunder inside me: Thou shalt not kill
But as I imagine that picture and the smiles therein
I think: For you my brothers, my sisters, my kin
For you I will

Wasted

I lie to myself
As I lie awake
Trying to breath
But each breathe that I take
Is just one more second ticking away
And the lie is translucent
I won't be okay
If each night and each day
That I find you away
Is nothing more than time
Wasted

I look around
At all the memories I've lost and found
It breaks my heart to run across them now
While I'm lonesome bound
But pain is nothing more than time
Wasted

What is life after all
If each time we stand up
We're just destined to fall
For the girl with the pretty blue eyes
Only to find that the days by her side
Were nothing but lies
And nothing more than time
Wasted

And suddenly
It's in a different light I see
This world in bitter clarity
All these years here between you and me
Undoubtedly
Are nothing more than time
Wasted

So I'll pour gasoline on this shoebox and strike the match
Watch the pictures and the trinkets catch
And hope
That just as grass
Can flourish amidst the embers and the ash
So can happiness
Rise up from the ruins of the past
And prove
That it wasn't simply time
Wasted

Who Cares?

What do you do when shit hits the fan?
What do you say when you haven't got a prayer?
How do you wake up from a five year plan?
And dreams so good that life is the nightmare?
Where do you turn when the road dead ends?
Where do you look when the lights go out?
Who do you seek when you haven't got any friends?
And you're so alone no one can hear you shout?
Who picks up the pieces?
Who wipes the tears?
Where's the shoulder to cry on?
Where's the ear for your fears?
Where's the soundboard?
The outlet?
The comfort?
Release?
Where's the shelter?
The sanctum?
The haven?
The peace?
How can you buck up or move on or bear it and grin?
How can you stand up and dust off and saddle up again?
Is there a method to madness?
To sorrow?
To pain?
Is there a blueprint to happiness?
To a pursuit not in vain?
What's the question?
The answer?
The riddle?
The scry?
What's the point?
The purpose?
The reason?

The why?
What's the who and the what and the when and the where?
And how?
After you broke my heart
After you left me here
With all these questions
With all these fears
How do I care?

Caged

You told me once of why you flinch
If I ever get too close
To someone other than yourself
As if I'd ever let you go
That fear of infidelity
You try so hard to hide
But all you do is hide yourself
Far away inside
I know of your little birdcage
And what you keep behind its bars
And why you even built it
And who drove you in so far
I know how much you loved her
And I know how much it hurt
That startling betrayal
So obscene and so overt
You couldn't face that torture
Or even risk a new romance
When someone else might do the same
If given a chance
So you locked yourself away
Made your pain a prison guard
Shaped your heart into a cell
And your ribs into the bars
Then you whiled away some years
Hoping scars could heal with time
But when you finally emerged
You found the sentence didn't fit the crime
So you fled back to your cage
You even fled from me
Thinking: "If this is freedom
Who would want to be free"
But I can hear your heartbeat
Fluttering in dismay

Frantic wingbeats that tell me
You want to fly away
You're tired of being trapped
More so than you fear
That if you fly too high
You'll burn up in the atmosphere
But Icarus flew in folly
With no destination to aim for
Where you have open arms
In which to soar
So fly my fallen angel
Soar my broken bird
I promise you won't fall again
Of that you have my word

Flown the Coop

I remember when all the floor was lava
And size six feet found purchase on
The igneous islands of discolored tiles
Skipping and hopping his way across the grocery store
He held his hat and cracked his plastic whip At snakes and spiders and crocodiles
Filling the cart with the plunders of a lost crypt
That only he could see
Treasures that looked suspiciously
Like cookies and candy to me
Those were the days he told me he loved me without prompting
And a hug was more than a customary embrace
When all his troubles were no bigger than he was
And a kiss could make any hurt go away
Now it isn't my kisses he seeks for comfort
Nor my arms he wraps his worries in
And any vocalizations of affection
He'll lavish on a lover before his kin
And I fear the day crawls in bed
With someone other than myself
Not fleeing nightmares as he used to do
But fleeing innocence itself
I watch him grow
Both up and away
And my heart soars
And my heart breaks
Because though I've spent all his life preparing him
To spread his wings and fly one day
I never did prepare myself
To watch him fly away

Curse of the Blank White Page

I used to write
Just for fun
My purposes?
I had none
But now I run
From line to line
Leaping words and turns of phrase
To try to find a way to say how much I hurt
To pour my pain into a pen
And pour it out upon a page
To weep, to rage, to hide away
Behind a wall of metaphors
And I abhor my loss of joy
The pleasure that I used too feel
In filling up a blank white page
With inky rhymes and doggerel
It seems my craft has fled my fingers
Fled my heart and mind as well
To hunker in the dark recess
Of shadowed shades I can't dispel
I'm no longer the puppeteer
Making words dance at my will
Now my heartstrings pull on me
And I must dance to feel
I cater to the laughing letters
Cower from the mocking verse
Scared of what they might reveal
Once my joy
Now my curse

The Book of Love

There was a boy who grew up reading fantasy
Where every character had a destiny
Love was in every story he'd ever read
And somewhere along the way he started to believe
That to live
That was all he'd ever need

Well that boy grew and he grew and he learned
That life didn't fit in the bindings of books
And love
Well sometimes it burned
But he kept growing both inside and and out
And he kept holding his hand over the fires of doubt
Daring the world to scorch him again
Or daring a girl to take it and prove
That books aren't just books in the end

The years rolled by and that boy lost his faith
As his hand lost feeling there over the flames
It blackened and burned and it shriveled away
Just like his heart and those books he'd stopped reading anyway
He watched those around him
Less devoted than he
Laughing and living and loving apparently
While he stayed alone
God it hurt just to live
And that's when he thought
Maybe death
Was better than this

Oh there was a girl
Who wrote her own songs
Trying to fill the hole where her heart had been long long ago

She sang of love lost and of love never found
She dove into the notes hoping sometimes she'd drown
And two doors away, if only she knew
A boy no longer a boy was drowning too

That's when he heard it
Faint in his ear
The sound of hope in the sound of despair
He dropped the blade
And made his way down the hall
Where the music promised he wasn't alone after all
He reached out a hand
And knocked on the door
The music stopped and all he could hear was the fire's roar
The boy saw the girl and the girl saw the boy
The fire didn't burn and the waters didn't drown her voice
She smiled at him and he smiled at her
And in the book of love another page turned

Lullaby

Rest
Your head now
Don't fret
I'm here
If nightmares try to plague your dreams I'll teach them how to fear
And if they refuse to yield
I shall be your sword and shield
Shining knight
Here to fight
Smiting those who wish you ill

This lullaby
I sing to thee
Let it put your mind at ease
Close your eyes
Count your sheep
Soon you will be fast asleep

The sandman is calling
He whispers in your ear
The dream scape is beckoning
You shouldn't linger here
A castle in the sky
Awaits for you to close your eyes
For torpor to transport you to another life

This lullaby
I sing to thee
Let it put your mind at ease
Close your eyes
Count your sheep
Soon you will be fast asleep

Escape
From reality
It cannot bind you here
Embrace
Imagination
I promise I'll be near
These soothing sounds will take you
They'll swaddle you in downy notes
So sink into the tender tones
In slumber you shall float

This lullaby
I sing to thee
Let it put your mind at ease
Close your eyes
Count your sheep
Soon you will be fast asleep

Purple Hearts

Everyone has wounds that don't quite heal
And every scar has a story it can tell
I've my fair lot to share myself
It's true
And every one of them
Begins with you
Love is a battlefield
And we're all soldiers getting by
Dodging bombs and bullets
And just trying to survive
But when the friend who fights beside you
Turns out to be the enemy
There is no medic here who can save me
I've thought about just throwing down my gun
Giving up the fight
While there's still something to be won
And then I look around and there I see
Wounded soldiers everywhere still fighting
We're all just purple hearts
Damaged goods still marching on
Finding comfort in our kindred pain
Our battered bond
And if my fellow soldiers
Can still heft their swords and fight
Them I can take my pen in hand
And write

Trust Issues

I said he picked me from my cherry tree
But that was a lie
I'm just an Asop's fable
I've got secrets to hide
A poisoned past
Unfertile soil
I'm not a place to plant
The seed of budding love
That he is searching for
I can't
I have been that blooming flower
Home to butterflies and rosy cheeks
And I have been the withered stalk
Home to buzzing flies and lesser things
So I will spare him me
Give him pleasure that a white lie brings
Make him think he's special for a night
And leave him memories
Before the poison seeps in
Before the axe bites deep
Before I see my pain reflected
In a gaze I cannot keep

An Exploration

Sheets are twisted underneath
Two bodies twisted in relief
Of growing wants and growing needs
Sating, slaking, planting seeds
Watering that fertile soil
Sweat stained skin, nocturnal toil
Fingers parting seas for pearls
Blooming flower now unfurled
My hands clasp upon your hips
My mouth is pressed against your lips
Your hands are clamped across your own
Stifling your mounting moans
Tremors in the hills and valleys
No time left to dillydally
Spring is nigh, the thaw has cum
Floodwaters flow upon my tongue
Mountains heave with quaking breaths
Hot flesh red with each caress
And all at once the trembling seizes
Breaths exhale in gentle breezes
Bodies crumple and deflate
As tensing muscles undulate
I crawl across your rosy flesh
Press my form to your undress
And there I feel the need still stirring
Gentle rumble, almost purring
Kisses press through flashing teeth
Soft and stiff meet in relief
And now the work begins in earnest
Coal heaved in a burning furnace
Locomotion as we steam
Toward lands unknown and worlds unseen

Genesis and Revelation

Our breath exhales like summer heat
Our skin melds like oceans meet
Our tongues dance like swaying wheat
A world forged beneath these sheets
Passion soars to mountain heights
Heartbeats flutter like birds in flight
Inhibition grows brittle, lust ignites
And the fires of ecstasy roar to life
Tender touches turn to raking
Pleasure giving turns to taking
Hunger feeding and thirst slaking
Fucking now, not mere lovemaking
Mountains crumble, forests burn
Oceans boil, storm clouds churn
Our world ends its short sojourn
Lust expends and love returns

Rage Quit

If life is a game
Then slip me the cheat codes
Infinite funds
Looks to match my libido
Give me an edge
Don't give me a handicap
Double xp and loot boosts
I'm down with that
I feel like I'm stuck
Been on this level forever
Progress reset
Let's co-op together
I've only got one life
Skills degrade without use
Eat, sleep, work, repeat
Man what's the use
I don't get the storyline
I don't see the goal
My princess is in another castle
This is getting old
I think I'm done, game over
Start, options, quit
Are you sure
Select yes and that's it

Fight

Word to my mother
Back talk
Trash talk
Thinking I'm adult with a sharp tongue
Half cocked
Loaded with insolence
Impudence and arrogance
Adolescent ego
Watch me go
Be independent
Stomping feet
Slamming doors
Voices raised to angry roars
I don't need you
I'm all grown up
I don't throw tantrums anymore
Control me
Hold me
Imprison me and smother
That's all you ever do
Like I'm a child, you, a mother
Somehow expendable
God I'm a fool
For I haven't got another

Shadows and Sunbeams

The sun brushed the horizon like a matchstick
And lit the sky aflame
Clouds of orange and red and gold
Blazed in brilliance, fire untamed
It licked across the stratosphere
In pace with the dying day
And in its wake the shadows stirred
Eager to come out and play
She stood there in that dying light
Half her face in darkness
The other wreathed in sunbeams
Contrast awing in its starkness
A smile played upon her lips
But quickly sank into a frown
Distant eyes glazed wet with pain
Hair tumbled as her head dipped down
Streaks of fire split her cheeks
Where tear tracks caught the light
A hand came up to grasp her chest
And shudders wracked her slender height
The flames began to dwindle down
Though clouds still burned like embers glowing
Fending off encroaching night
The shadows ever growing
They swallowed up her sorrowed features
Painting grey her pretty face
The beauty faded with the light
Till only anguish stood in place
That was when at last I reached her
Cross the darkened yard
My arms wrapped tight around her womb
Squeezing tight, but not too hard
She hardly seemed to register
The contact through her trembling

But patience won me cognizance
Her sundered thoughts assembling
The last pale glimmers of the sun
Had given way to total night
Our eyes adjusted to the change
Pupils large in search of light
A cool breeze blew about her shoulders
Tossing hair haphazardly
She shivered this time from the cold
Turned and burrowed into me
I felt my shirt grow wet with tears
But felt little price to pay
If I could dry her eyes for good
And keep the pain at bay
I placed a kiss upon her pate
And held her chin between soft fingers
Then lifted her eyes to my own
And saw that hurt still lingered
A gentle pressure tilted more
Her gaze to greater heights
Where the inky blackness of the sky
Lay spackled thick with lights
We watched them for an untold time
Till necks began to ache
Then rested foreheads brow to brow
No tension there to break
She broke the contact first and said
Confusion in her eyes
"I do not understand"
Clearly referencing the sky
I smiled at her and I said
"No matter how dark any night"
I pointed at the stars above
"At the edge of every shadow there is light"

Paragon

How do you choose
Between what you've lost
And what you've still got to lose
And how do you know
Which way to go
When the path that you've walked
Hits a fork in the road
And how do you carry on
When everything is gone
But you refuse to let it go

The past may be a burden
But the future's looking weighty too
And my back is breaking
From this heavy heart and all its been through
I try to shed some pounds
Through blood and sweat and mostly tears
But all I ever seem to lose
Are smiles and sleep and years
And I'm getting older
With no best days yet to leave behind
The only greater enemy than me I have it seems
Is time

I'm getting desperate
For love and purpose and destiny
Every protagonist in every story I like
Is now younger than me
My dreams are drifting
Further out of reach
And I'm much too tired these days
To match their speed
I need some inspiration
Someone to urge me on
Someone with a wake worth riding
I need a paragon

Murphy's Law

I tossed rocks at your window
In the middle of the night
They shattered the glass
And you called the cops
That's the story of my life

Scared

I don't know whether to hit things
Or to curl up and cry
To let you go with band-aid haste
Or hold on for dear life
Should I burn my bridges
Will the flames take me as well
Or can time bring us closer
As sure as the continents themselves
I feel as if I'm drowning
But the breaths still come and go
Am I truly falling
Or is that just vertigo
I'm walking this dark tunnel
Unsure if it has an end
Should I turn back or could there be
Light just around the bend
All these doubts and questions
Still no answers to be found
And I am growing weaker
Can I survive another round
Or will the count be called
The time and date declared
Am I dying or is this living
Either way I'm truly scared

Sidelines

I can see the struggle
It's written on your face
In worry lines and red eyes
Where two worlds war for space
Your heart beats out its battle march
It's calling you to fight
For you're in love and love is worth
Most any sacrifice
But in your soul another anthem
Sounds its own distress
As love would have you trample on
All other happiness
To leave behind the kind of life
You feel you're meant to live
You may receive so much from her
But is it more than you would give
The bombshells burst behind your eyes
And I can see the damage
This war is causing you more pain
Than you were built to manage
And here I am with answers
With compromise and resolution
But I cannot win wars for you
Through unwanted revolution
So I sit back and watch and wait
And sob to see the pain you're in
Hoping that your war ends soon
Before there's nothing left to win

Reborn

I want to bruise your lips with kisses
Wrap your fingers tight in mine
Let my heart tell you I love you
In staccato thumps that beat in time
With ragged breaths and shaky limbs
And bodies syncing rhythms
As our eyes lock with each other's
White light shining through a prism
I can see the colors bursting forth
In chocolate hair and blushing cheeks
Shadows casting angles
On the curves of your physique
Dainty sounds escape your lips
Gruff ones pass through mine
As heated flesh and lust and love
All meet and intertwine
Waves on rocks can't match our melding
Now our bodies move in tandem
Heat and gooseflesh war for province
Seemingly at random
I feel my pleasure rising up
No calm before this storm
Lightning flash and thunder clash
Once two, now one, reborn

Nostalgia

Sometimes I still find your hair in my bed
The scent of you lingers
Like words left unsaid
I twirl that golden thread
Soft between fingers
And breathe deep that coconut oil shampoo
It takes me back years
To that first day we met
Long before tears would be stifled or wept
You left a wake of paradise promises
Vows that would never be kept
Neither by me or by you

Falling

I saw you and I fell for you
I took your hand and you fell too
We fell for years
But one day you stopped
And I didn't
The distance between us grew and grew
And I fell and fell and fell apart
And then I stopped too
For a long time I stayed there
In suspended animation
Brought lower than I'd ever been before
Sometimes others fell past me
And I let their reaching hands fall
Untouched
I did not want to fall again
And so one day I began climb
My progress began slow
I made little headway
But my strength grew as I rose
Inch by inch
Each its own struggle
But getting easier
And suddenly I found myself
On level ground again
Stronger than I'd been last I was there
But now I wasn't sure what to do
There was nowhere left to rise
No new heights to claim
Just level ground to pass my days
And the old fall beckoning
I stared into that depth
And from it emerged a hand
A familiar hand
I grasped it and pulled you up

And here we were again
Same place, but new people
Holding each other up
Instead of pulling each other down
I'll never need to fall again

Singed

Find me in the rubble
With soot stained face and stubble
Bloody fingers sifting through
The wreck of me and you
I'm searching for a memory
A single moment shared by we
Two clueless kids who knew naught of
The darker side of love
For any candle burning bright
Casts shadows stark against its light
And when the wax has dripped its last
Those shadows move in fast
I'm sitting in that dark
Trying to spark my burnt out heart
But I'm only singing fingers
The warmth fades fast but the pain lingers
The cold is creeping, sharp and cruel
And I'm almost out of fuel

Desperate

I need to ask you something
But I'm not sure what
Any excuse to hear your voice
That ought to be enough
I try to space out my messages
To not sound overbearing
But I'm eager in the silent stretches
To know how you are faring
I guess you can call my clingy
Wanting to fill every moment with you
But when I'm my only company
Hey, I've got a question for you

Tide

I've got a heart full of problems
That I want you to see
But I always end up smiling
Whenever you look at me
The tears stay bottled up
Until the minute you leave
Then that hidden heart of mine
Alights upon my sleeve
The butterflies that fluttered
Grow heavy in my gut
And all that pain you held in check
Seeps out through a cut

Rock Bottom

I feel myself falling
No handholds in sight
I shouldn't have jumped
But it felt so right
And rocks bottom's approaching
To break my fall
And break my heart
And break my resolve
It's a familiar place
Where fragments abound
Of past mistakes
That jut like knives from the ground
Just waiting to pierce me
To skewer and slice
My peace of mind to pieces
And my heart back down to size
An empty place
That feels too much like home
Populated by so many lost loves
Yet where I am most alone

War-torn

There's a fine line between a man and a monster
Though alike in the number they've killed
There's a clear cut divide between hero and villain
Though equal in blood that they've spilled
There's a difference between you and me don't you see
Though we stand on the same battlefield
Because where you fight for glory and live by the sword
I only live by the shield
There is no honor in war that is fought
In a land that you do not call home
You are not uplifting nor freeing a people
Like some post-modern Empire of Rome
We did not invite you to fix all our problems
By killing our misguided sons
Change comes with time and the lessons it teaches
Not through your bombs and your guns
So leave us alone to struggle and rise
From the rubble of many mistakes
Because freedom that's earned will long be remembered
Unlike that which is given away

The Queen of Hearts

This kingdom belongs to the Queen of hearts
But I would dare to take it
To swipe the scepter from her hand
And on the cobbles break it
She may rule from leagues away
With a claim cemented in history
But leaders claim with more than words
And words are my weapons you see
It isn't that I bear her hostility
It's merely that she should not stake
This land here as her own to keep
With no commitment to it's uptake
And I guess she sensed that weakness
For now she's moving in
Tightening her hold on this heartland
And driving me out from within
Now the Queen may be strong in her castle
But though brick and mortar shut me out
A rebel has his ways to fight
To enter and from her throne do route
For if she is the Queen of Hearts
Then I am the King of Spades
And I will entrench myself before this gate
For however long it takes

Road Rage

I've got my head bowed
Face pale as a bedsheet
Nothing but ripped jeans
Between my knees and the concrete
I've got blood on my hands
Got mud on my feet
Got pain in my heart
Got tears on my cheeks
I can feel the adrenaline pumping
Shock keeps me locked in place
But heart's thumping
Jumping from one beat to the next
Symptom of my post-traumatic stress
There's a body right in front of me
Lifeless, cold, unrecognizably
You
I can't see the laughter in your eyes
Color drained and flesh as cold as ice
Face is frozen, look is horrified
Finger pointed, blames and identifies
Me
Your murderer

I Could

I sit alone in a parked car
Warm engine and a cold heart
My mind is drifting but it's not far
From you
My fingers fiddle with that old key
The one I gave you but you didn't keep
Vison blurring and I can't see
The truth
Is this time wasted or time saved
My one chance squandered or another made
Is your love dormant or did it really fade
For good
Pound my frustrations into the steering wheel
Rip my wounds wider than they're ever like to heal
Should I silence this pain I feel
I could

Cardiac Conversion

Lay down your arms
Drop your guard
You don't need an army
To shelter your heart
You can trust me
To give it good care
I'll give you my own
And call the trade fair
Then maybe you'll realize
Then maybe you'll see
That my heart beats as much for you
As it ever has for me

Partners in Crime

Lay your head upon my shoulder
Lay your problems at my feet
I'll do my best to drive the demons from your soul
Though I've no angel's wings
And I my fail
And I may fall
And I may join you on that headstone
But I'll be damned
If I'll stand by
And let you face the dark alone

Grey Paint

I feel as alive as a musician
And as dead as a poet
My music speaks of joy
But my lyrics don’t know it
They undermine and undercut
And darken the picture
Grey paint on the palette
Seeping into every mixture
I’m a verdant valley
With storm clouds above
Because in every broken heart
Once, there was love

Twisted Lullaby

Tears wet my pillow
Snot stains my sheets
Fists strangle cotton
I shake like a leaf
I flit between anger
And sorrow and gloom
Too many emotions
Become too little too soon
The emptiness fills
And then empties again
Like waves upon rocks
Wearing me thin
And finally, blessedly
Fatigue settles in
Then sleep subtly shrouds me
And the nightmares begin

Feet First

I know that people are grey
All black and white and in between
But I like to think that if you get close
More colors can be seen
Veins of blue and hearts of red
And souls of rainbow hues
Where light and shadow interplay
To make me me and make you you
And I know it can be dangerous
For people surely bite
And a trusting person like myself
Is tempting to any anthropomagite
But I'd rather be a delicacy
Than a bitter pill to swallow
Grating against society
Paranoid and hollow
So I'll keep putting my neck on the line
Trusting too easy and loving too deep
Risking it all for a toss of a coin
Heads and it kills me, tails and I reap
The rewards of a friendship
And perhaps more some day
Because I saw color
Where others saw grey

Happy Valentines

I took her to the overlook
And pushed her off the edge
Because that's what cheaters deserve

Moral of the Story

I am Atlas and you're my itchy nose
I'm Tantalus and you're the water
Lapping at my toes
I am Prometheus
You are the vulture
I am Pygmalion
You, my sculpture
I am Dionysus
You're the sour grape
I am Narcissus
And you are my lake
I am Pandora and you're in the box
I am Sisyphus on the hill
And you're my rolling rock
I am Persephone
You're the pomegranate
I'm the myth
You're the monster
That's our story dynamic

Laughter

White teeth, red lips
Crescent curve of happiness
Deepened dimples, nose twitch
Crinkled eyes and side stitch
Pale flesh, painted pink
Tousled hair tumbling
Round your shoulders and your face
Shuddering, bent at the waist
Gasping breaths, hands clasping sides
Reactions of a tickle fight

War and Peace

There's this girl I see from time to time
That you might find familiar
Every time that you look in a mirror
A battleground sits in my heart
Where battle drums beat me apart
And smoke obscured emotions remain unclear

I look deep and recognize The same war raging in your eyes
Every time you cast a glance my way
Bombshells burst within your head
You're blinded, deafened, left for dead
Reason somehow lost within the fray

We try to stop and bunker down
Entrench ourselves on safer ground
Hesitant to kick the hornets' nest
Content to wait and siege it out
Clear the smoke, erase the doubt
But neither can resist an offensive test

War is hell, but so is love
And all is fair when both of us
Are fighting just to gain an upper hand
Propaganda, slander, and
Contriving covert stratagems
Suppressing feelings we don't understand

Some soldiers fall, some soldier on
Battles lost and battles won
But war is just an action with a cause
Peace and love and happiness
The search for one to share it with
And fight for when the peal of duty calls

A Clockwork Heart

You cannot wind me if I stutter
I do not have a clockwork heart
If it stops, it stops for good
And your love was the start

Miles

This chain
It pulls
It pulls upon my heart
A new link
Adds to its length
Each inch we drift apart
Seems my defense is far from flawless
For while it keeps our two hearts tethered
Even if we're not together
The weight can grow and swell and burgeon
No heart is meant to bear such burden
Without breaking from the stress
And now you're stepping on a plane
I brace my feet and grasp the chain
Prepared for your departure
But as you take off down the runway
Promising "I'll see you someday"
That chain is flying from my chest
And its weight is crushing at best
Mere moments and it's torture
I guess that's why love rarely lasts
When distances grow far too vast
For even Atlas must have shrugged
And shook his head in pity
To see the weight I bore the day
You left for New York City

Shut Out

You put so much effort into erecting that wall around your heart
And now you're trying so hard to tear it apart
But you're just casting glass at a stone house
All your attacks just break against the brick and now
You've found that you're trapped in your own protective layer
A pawn in the game of your life, instead of a player
And you're losing

Firing Blanks

Lock and load an empty chamber
Pull the trigger, nix the danger
Fire blanks into my skull
To feel some semblance of control
Forget about fate and destiny
Tangled strings and puppetry
Master plans are far too long
A million ways they might go wrong
I would rather take the reins
Spur my charge, break my chains
Live my life from day to day
Make the best of all that comes my way
And if I stumble in my journey
No roads forward or returning
I'll pitch my tent there in the lull
And fire blanks into my skull

A Modest Proposal

I tried everything that I could think to try
But nothing I can do will change your mind
You've set your course
With no remorse
For leaving me behind
You say I can't give you everything you need
But I've given you everything
I've got to lose
You can't have your cake and eat it too
Are you so blind
Can't I just be enough for now
A little part of the whole you want from life somehow
That's more than you've got left
After leaving all the rest
In the past
You don't have to give me much
A little love will be enough
To satisfy
Everything I want from life
That's all I ask

Seasons of a Broken Heart

Tears rain down like leaves in Autumn
Leaving hearts and branches bare
And cold creeps in like apathy
Casting doubt that Summer was ever there
And though I know that Spring approaches
To bloom new love in fertile earth
Winter seems an endless span
Of bitter winds and icy hurt

Corpse Bride

I buried you in your wedding dress
To cheat Death of his satisfaction
For you've never looked more alive

Comeuppance

I hope I'm there when he hurts you And you've nowhere to go
So I can turn my back too
And tell you I told you so

Writer's Block

I don't know what to write about
Though my emotions churn like storm tossed seas
For while words stream steadily from my pen
They've no subject of which to speak
So I ramble out rhymes
And I scribble out script
And the page fills up
But it's an empty manuscript
I see no piece of me pressed on the paper
No personal portrait etched into the letters
Beautiful, eloquent, well-structured trash
An illiterate fool could write better

The Price of Pride

I tried to bite my tongue
But the words came pouring out
All those angry unsaid things
That I can't take back now
They leapt like lightning from my lips
Thunderous in their savagery
But I was more conductive
And they only wound up shocking me
It's stupid looking back now
Thinking I could patch things up
By tearing even greater rents
In the fabric of our love
Now you'd hardly recognize
That we were once each other's world
Closer than the finest stitch
Nigh on inseparable
Now my throat is raw from hate
My heart so scoured from shame
And of our one time vibrant, healthy love
Wounds are all that remain

Keep Your Friends Close

Look to the far horizon
See there the setting sun
Gaze past the misty mountains
Between you and there and farther still
All you see is one
Sprint through the endless forest
Bound across the ceaseless plain
Set sail over boundless waters
The view may alter, shift, or change
But the dirt beneath will always be the same
Seek out every hue and pigment
That paints a persons skin
Find every culture found then
Turn back and find you'll never find
A single one the same again
I can see past the walls and fences
Beyond the borders and the claims of men
I have watched the waving flags
And in every one I see
The colors of the wind
Look to the far horizon
Look to the distant stars
See the distance between grains of sand
And find that it's all just perspective
They're all as near and all as far
As you are from me

A Fairytale of Sorts

I rode in on an all-white stallion
Sunlight gleaming off my plate
Rapscallion smile and roguish charm
Plastered on my face
I must have looked the dashing hero
A prince charming come to save
The dough-eyed damsel in distress
A most impressive feat of daring
I must say
That's how I saw it in my head
Playing out without a hitch
A predilection of predicted triumph
After which I'd finally get the girl
But how could I predict the course
At which events would come to pass
That later would seem obvious
As disaster was most certain to unfurl
I should have known that stallions shit
As animals are wont to do
And armor in the summer heat
Would simmer me like stew
So I trotted in less confident
In the wake of stomach-churning scents
Of sweat and shame and horse manure
My armor full of dents
The iron shone just as I'd hoped
But straight into my eyes so that
I lost my balance in the saddle
And fell right on my ass
Mortified I was to hear
Though barely heard above the pounding
Of my hotly burning shame
Your ringing laughter sounding

I tried to fall back in retreat
To save what pride I might have left
But in my clanging, clanking haste
My helmet tumbled off my head
I hid my face as best I could
To cling to anonymity
Staring daggers at the dirt
In hopes you knew not my identity
But from the corner of my eye
An outstretched hand came into view
And my name whispered in my ear
From lips I'd hoped to woo
I raised my head in mute surprise
And took the hand presented
And, with your help, regained my feet
My plan successful in the end
If not how I'd intended
And finally I pulled you close
With dignity regained
Into a kiss of timeless length
A fairytale of sorts
I can't complain

Savior

I am my own worst enemy
And I don't know how to face me
I am the monster I don't want to be
And I don't know to break free
So I'm calling out to a higher power
To stand where I can only cower
And be a savior

Take my body, take my soul
Won't you show me where to go
I need a savior
Take my heart, take my hand
Be my footsteps in the sand
I need a savior

There's so much darkness in the world
Black and white together swirled
Bathing life in darkened shades of gray
And I'll admit I've cast my shadow in the fray
So who will rise as our messiah
Not I, unclean, impure, pariah
But a savior

Help me stand, help me see
Part the waters for me
I need a savior
Teach me wrong, teach me right
Won't you show me the light
I need a savior

I've yet to see a worthy man
Rise above and make a stand
To lead the way into the light
So I guess I'll have to try to lead the fight

I'll take the steps wash my soul
Clean of sin, renewed, and whole
Perhaps a savior

Because I can walk and I can see
And I can talk and I can lead
And I can fight and I can plead
And I can live and I can breathe
And I can die and I can bleed
And I can rise and I can be
A savior

A Day in the Life of Depression

I wake to shadows in my eyes
It's 4 am, still dark outside
Tear streaks on my pillow prove
That even sleep can't perk my mood
Burnt coffee and a cigarette
Shower, shave, and introspect
Inhale, exhale, steady breaths
Motions like a marionette
I slip into my second skin
Don my happy face again
Twinkling eyes and pleasant grin
Slapped across the bleak and grim
Nine to five, daily grind
Lock myself inside my mind
Familiar monsters lie in wait
My sanity upon their plate
Punch the clock, ditch the mask
Stereo turned up full blast
Make it home, draw the blinds
Free the monsters from my mind
Until the sun no longer shines
Pause the tape, then hit rewind

Arousing Tale

She was oil, I was water
Take a guess who was on top
Sheen of her skin grown slick
Mouthing "Don't stop"
Hair all a jumble
Tumbled locks like a silk screen
Give her my confession
Sinning as I wipe my slate clean
Hot flesh underhand
I melt into a puddle
Coalesce to a climax
Anything but subtle
As I groan like branches
Bending in a strong wind
She moans like a gale
It's hurricane season
And I just found
The eye of the storm
Chaos surrounds
Two placid forms

Anthropomorphism

My trust is a deer in the city
Ears pricked and swiveled in constant alert
Eyes wide and legs coiled
Skittish and terrified, ready to bolt

My heart is a turtle in heat
Roaming in need, but always walled in
Constantly ready to receive or recede
Slow and steady, but ready to win

My mind is a clam in the bustling sea
Alive inside but outwardly still
My thoughts are racing, raging within
Pearls forming beneath my shell

My hope is a lion on the African plains
Roaming the heath that is my domain
Hunting for sustenance, hunted for sport
My kingship contested upon the food chain

My love is a bee in a garden
Searching for beautiful petals to land
To give and take, symbiotic connection
But stinger at the ready for uncaring hands

Fear of the Light

I first saw you in the dark of night
With fingers that traced curves without judgement
With lips that tasted stretch marks and scars without disgust
Blushes did not blemish, but only warmed your skin
You let inhibition go and cast off insecurities to pool next to your clothes
You revealed yourself to me in tremors and gasps
Gave yourself to me without regret
But in the morning it was different
I kissed you and you shied away
Hid beneath the satin sheets
You turned your back to don your clothes
And would not look me in the eye
You trusted the dark more than me to find you beautiful
And I began to wonder who had hurt you so
That the only mirror in your possession was only big enough to show your face
And that all your clothes had the tags ripped out
You kept the lighting low and the curtains long
Hiding from a world you feared would judge
If only you could step in my shoes and see through my eyes
You'd know the only one judging you
Is you

Perfect Storm

You catch my gaze with eyes of mischief
Full of need and all permissive
Beckoning me to come hither
I need no moment to consider
I push you down onto the bed
My own need rising like the dead
And mold myself into your figure
Pulse pounding in my loins with rigor
I feel the heat of lust there growing
Tight beneath the fabric showing
And you must have felt it too
For soon your hands my fly undo
You bare me to your naked flesh
I pull you close until I'm pressed
My solid lust against wet lips
In loose resemblance of a kiss
Then like a fresh blade quenched and tempered
I douse myself into your whimpers
Cries of joy as fingers rake
Across my back in pleasure's wake
The passion builds in pace and volume
I an island, you a monsoon
I ride the storm, the storm rides me
A merging of land and sky and sea
Till we are one become our pleasure
Lost within the raging weather

Stalemate

I never thought those little things
Would mean so much to me
But now they're gone for good
And they are all that I can't see
You have changed so much
You're not the person that you were
And I can't love this new you
Because I'm still in love with her
And you could even say
That I am just a hypocrite
For I have changed as much and more
And I'm not all the better for it
Sure, we can both point fingers
Or bear the burden of the blame
But in the end it will not quench
Our bridges wreathed in flame
We both watch the fire
From different edges of a chasm
It yawns between our empty hearts
Smoke billowing phantasms
Neither wants to be the first
To turn our back upon the other
And admit through action
That we might have been the lesser lover
So we sit in stalemate
Neither clear on course of action
More alike than we could know
In our dissatisfaction

The Storm in the Night

I try to pull myself together
As close as I can
Like any appendage extended
Might break off in the whirlwind
Of emotions surrounding me
Raw and intense
My fetal position seems feeble
A flimsy defense
Like I might fly apart
At the slightest disturbance
I am equilibrium
But you are discordance
You come all a jumble
Of sense and sensation
Palpable memories
Pure manifestation
And I lie there trembling
In the eye of the storm
Betwixt tear stained sheets
And pillows deformed
The banshee winds wail
Past the lump in my throat
Until sorrow strangles me
Like a garrote
My thundering heart
Crashes loud in my ears
Till its crescendo tempo
Is all I can hear
I don't know when the storm
Ceased and abated
Or when I succumbed to fatigue
And deflated
But when I awoke
To the sun shining bright

It seemed clearer for enduring
The storm in the night

New Age

Oh I want to three a B
See the pattern?
Skipping rocks on the Moon
Tossing rings on Saturn
Caught in a landslide
I can't find the bottom
Of the bottle in my liver
Dropped the balls
Then caught 'em
No I won't grow up
Lost boy mentality
Empty wallet
That's harsh reality
The dreamers die young
Or they wake up fast
Be the first to the worm
Or you'll wind up last
From the cherry red glow
Of my final cigarette
I swear I'll quit
Then dance like a marionette
Two packs later
Still swear I'm not addicted
Gotta hit that high
So I don't feel conflicted
Signed up for all my college classes
But I won't show up
Because I paid my taxes
And the system failed
To return my investment
Now I can't afford the time
Or my antidepressants
So I'll pass my days
Trading sleep for paper

Until a zombie walk
Usurps my caper
And I'll fill my nights
Filling pages with poetry
Until I run out of rhymes

A Rock and a Hard Place

I have been to the bottom of the barrel
In the bottom of the bottle
At the bottom of the pile
Where it felt familiar after a while
Sinking under worries stacked on anxieties
Where the only that's rising is my bile
Yeah I've been in the lonely dark
With nothing but a broken heart
Counting all my fortunes on one hand
Pennies filling up a jar
Slower than the bottom of
The hourglass is filling up with sand
And still I say

Everything will be alright
Everything will be ok
Everything will turn out right someday
Everything will be just fine
If I put in work
If I put in time
Because if there's a will then there's a way

Sometimes words drip from my fingers
From my tongue
And from my pen
And nothing that they say
Is worth the time it takes to read them
Pointless drivel, no cohesion
Full of rhyme, but not of reason
Letters strung together on a whim
And I begin to doubt my purpose
Doubt my skill
And doubt my right
To write when everything I write is wrong

Till I must take a big step back
And take a breath until I'm calm
And say

Everything will be alright
Everything will be ok
Everything will turn out right someday
Everything will be just fine
If I put in work
If I put in time
Because if there's a will then there's a way

Just Do It

Imagine a place where a bad crop means more than simple inflation
It means starvation
Where the inclination to be more than an imitation of your mother or father is grounds for excommunication
Where overtime is breaking even and vacation is a nursery rhyme
Imagine for a moment that just imagining something better is a crime
But you don't have to imagine it
You can find it right here
Down the dusty road and across the pond
We call it backwards or third world
But they're not living in rewind
We just live in a different society
Fed on the anti-sobriety of fast pace and borrowed time
It isn't that we're selfish
We're simply blind
Like race horses with tunnel vision that know only how to reach the finish line
The line that divides us from reality and where we want to be
The truth is that we're just as backwards as the rest
Self-confessed in our addiction for a fictional world where we're the best of the best
We're obsessed with a complex that the world is more complex than we're willing to admit
That crunching numbers is somehow more useful than shoveling shit
And shit doesn't taste better off a silver spoon
Nor do we have more right to walk the Earth because we walked on the moon
Maybe we should spend less time touting our success
And nursing our regrets
And spend more time tackling our upsets

The problems still proving problematic in the present
While we throw tantrums like entitled kings and entitled peasants
Is it really so hard to see room to improve
That we'd rather pretend that it doesn't exist than to actually move
To progress towards a future greater than today
Instead of passing from year to year pressing rewind and replay
Are we so scared of being un-unique that we'd rather be wrong
Rather stick to a flawed system than play along
Like a child rubbing his new toy in another's face
Just because that same kid beat him in a foot race
It isn't relevant, but it's all he's got
We're irrelevant, but we pretend we're not
We polish our trophies and say look how great we are
And the world says look how great you were
Maybe it's time to polish our shoes instead
And prove that we can still be winners

We The People

I'm standing in the classroom
Got my hand over my heart
Reciting words full of bullet holes
Under God?
Think not
One nation, of the people
Not the bank, not the steeple
Think we're all created equal?
Think again
Hate is legal
If you haven't got a cross in your heart
Hope to die
Because we're under the thumbs
Of the rich, religious, white guys
And I think it's time we faced it
That our country's not the greatest
We got cop killers killing cops
Cops killing cop killers
Innocents caught in the crossfire
Cops fire, not fired
Fires in the streets
Torches in the hands
Media spreading mass hysteria
Across the lands
We've got race wars
Class wars
No middle class
Just rich and poor
We still base our power
On the dower found beneath the belt
Bigotry, Idolatry
To Reagan or to Roosevelt
We've got no middle ground
Got no middle man

Binary lateral heads buried in the sand
Red blood, blue blood
Flinging shit, raking mud
Wash it all away
In the waters of the second Flood
We're just debt ridden war mongers
No longer on top
Who can't seem to cope with our loss of the head spot
Spot light, too bright
Couldn't take the pressure
Now the pressure cooker's cooking
For this third world oppresser
This oil war aggressor
This shining beacon built upon the backs of the lesser
And those backs, they're not breaking
They've grown strong for their burdens
And they're rising up now
To strike down this perversion
Of a sorry excuse for a land of liberty
This waste of potential
For freedom and equality
Of the people
By the people
For the people
Please
You only count as people
If you aren't a minority

Effeuiller la Marguerite

Petals filter through her fingers
She loves her so, she loves her not
They tumble like lost opportunities
Till a withered stalk is all she's got
She clutches her last option
Between her index and her thumb
Gripped so tight in yearning
That her hand is going numb
A bouquet, now one flower shy
She holds against a heaving chest
A shaking finger rings the doorbell
Fight or flight put to the test
Her head is a spool of memories
Upon her heart reflected
Flickers of nostalgic light
Past moments recollected
Of ocean eyes and chocolate locks
Caramel skin beneath her fingers
Sundress swishing round smooth calves
Where the scent of spice still lingers
So tangible the reverie
And lost amidst the reminiscence
She fails to note the open door
And silent form there present
But sudden heat blooms in her cheeks
And a tightness tugs beneath her breast
Drawing her attention forth
To she who smiles in silent jest
Sea-foam eyes take in the flowers
Endless depths revealing naught
Is there judgement in that stare?
Pity? Passion? Prudent thought?
She can feel her fingers shaking
As she lifts the flowers forth

Her voice reflecting their vibrations
Booming on that silent porch
Three small words with such big meaning
Hang there in the space between
Where the scent of daisies fills the void
Of professed love still echoing
And then the waves return to shore
That ocean gaze now overflowing
Onto cheeks and into lips
Upturned now in joyous knowing
Flowers press between their bodies
In remembrance of the day
As she meets her lips in answer
Chocolate hair in disarray
Petals crumple underfoot
Long forgotten, soft winds blow
A single brethren drops to join them
And there says, she loves her so

Night-lights

Ever since I was a little girl
I've always loved the stars
Counting constellations
Watching worlds spin so far away
But it's been years
Since I've ventured the night
What I wouldn't give
Not to fear for my life
Just to walk down the street
Beneath winking eyes
Old friends that don't criticize
When I jump at every shadow
And shy from every stranger
Always so guarded
From every lurking danger
It didn't used to be so
But I met a monster on this street
He took me from the lights
And showed just how dark the dark can be
So now I watch the stars
Through dead bolts and double panes
Marshaling my strength
Taking steps and making gains
My wounds are closing
Even if the scars won't fade
I will stand beneath those stars again
Some night someday

Id to Ego

She feels like a poor painting
In a gallery of fine art
Patrons pointing, judging
Leaving less than kind remarks
"Paint's thin here, but too thick there
And look at that complexion
It must have been a shaky hand
That gave that brush direction"
And all around her, hanging, mocking
Portraits of the highest class
Saying "You're unworthy" and
"You're fit for naught but trash"
And she's believing every word
She's taking them to heart
Till colors bleed down canvas cheeks
And all her tones turn dark
But all the while she's forgetting
The gallery's in her head
In reality it's just a mirror
Mocking in its stead

I am the Aftermath

I was the muffled curses through the bedroom walls
I was the shattered glass in the slamming door
I was the tension in the silent meals
I was the empty bottles on the living room floor
I was the rip in the wedding pictures
I was the midnight calls to the cops
I was the trip to the in-law's house
I was the belongings in the first moving box
I was the letters from two different lawyers
I was the gavel in the final decree
I was the loss and the victory
I was the displaced fruit of two barren trees
I was the son
That you tore in two
I did not kill myself
That guilt lies on you

Ruins

Any old thing can start a war
But only love can truly end it
I've been at war for many years
All thoughts of peace suspended
I've battled for my every beat
This broken heart defended
I'm begging someone to break through
And with three words so mend it

Author's Note

I would like to give a big shout-out to all my friends, family, followers, and fans for making this book possible. Not only did you deal with the emotional rollercoaster that gave depth to my poetry, but many of you were there offering advice, editing, and input whenever it was needed, some from the start and many more along the way. Thank you all for your contributions however large or small they may have been. All of them were important steps on the journey. Now, I may have reached my destination, but I have no intentions of stopping here. I have many more avenues left to explore and I hope you'll all be there with me to discover them together.

Sincere Thanks,
Devon Eaton

Made in the USA
San Bernardino, CA
18 September 2017